New and Selected Poems

David Wagoner

New and Selected Poems

Indiana University Press   *Bloomington London*

SECOND PRINTING 1970

Published in Canada by Fitzhenry & Whiteside Limited,
Scarborough, Ontario

Library of Congress catalog card number: 69-16002

Manufactured in the United States of America

SBN 253-15770-6 cloth   253-29934-4 paper

For Patt with love, new and unselected

CONTENTS

7

from Staying Alive *(1966)*

New Poems

9

ACKNOWLEDGMENTS

The new poems in this book appeared in the following periodicals in the years shown: "Speech from a Comedy, II," "Bums at Breakfast," "Recollection," "The Hold-up," 1967, and "In the Open Season," "Weather Report," "Nine Charms Against the Hunter," "Searching in the Britannia Tavern," "Crossing Half a River," 1968, HUDSON REVIEW; "Tumbleweed," "The Escape Artist," "The Soles," "One for the Sun, One for the Moon," 1966, and "Stretching," "Learning to Swim," 1967, and "Short Story," "Fire by the River," 1969, SATURDAY REVIEW; "The March of Coxey's Army," "Getting Out of Jail on Monday," "Getting Above Ourselves on Sunday," "Archeological Notes," 1967, and "The Apotheosis of the Garbagemen," "Note from Body to Soul," "Ceremony on Pier 40," 1969, POETRY; "Blues to be Sung in a Dark Voice," "Magic Night at the Reformatory," 1967, THE NATION; "The Shoplifter," 1968, THE JOURNAL OF CREATIVE BEHAVIOR; "At St. Vincent DePaul's," 1966, and "Plainsong for Everyone Who Was Killed Yesterday," 1969, THE NEW YORKER; "The Burglar," 1966, CHICAGO REVIEW; "The Visiting Hour," "The Warbler," "Last Look," 1969, KAYAK.

The poems from *A Place to Stand*, *The Nesting Ground*, and *Staying Alive* appeared originally in the following periodicals: *Poetry, Botteghe Oscure, New World Writing, New Poems, The New Yorker, Hudson Review, International Literary Annual, Saturday Review, The London Observer, The Massachusetts Review, Prairie Schooner, Choice, Southern Review, Minnesota Review, Yale Review, Northwest Review, Seattle Magazine, Poetry Northwest.*

from *A Place to Stand*
(1958)

To My Friend Whose Parachute Did Not Open

Thrown backwards first, head over heels in the wind
Like solid streamers from the wing to tail,
You counted whatever pulses came to mind—
The black, the bright—and at the third, you pulled,
Pulled savagely at the ring clenched in your hand.

Down the smooth slope of your trajectory,
Obeying physics like a bauble of hail,
Thirty-two feet per second per second hurled
Toward treetops, cows, and crouching gravity
From the unreasonable center of the world,

You saw the cords trail out from behind your back,
Rise up and stand, tied to a piece of cloth
Whose edges wobbled, but would not spread wide
To borrow a cup of air and hold you both.
O that tall shimmer whispered you were dead.

You outraced thought. What good was thinking then?
Poor time—no time for plunging into luck
Which had, like your whirling, weightless flesh, grown thin.
I know angelic wisdom leaped from your mouth,
But not in words, for words can be afraid:

You sang a paean at the speed of sound,
Compressed miraculous air within your head
And made it fountain upward like a cowl.
And if you didn't, then you struck the ground.
And if you struck the ground, both of us died.

Words Above a Narrow Entrance

The land behind your back
Ends here: never forget
Signpost and weathercock
That turned always to point
Directly at your eyes;
Remember slackening air
At the top of the night,
Your feet treading on space.
The stream, like an embrace,
That swamped you to the throat
Has altered now; the briar
Rattling against your knees,
The warlock in disguise,
The giant at the root—
The country that seemed
Malevolence itself
Has gone back from the heart.

Beyond this gate, there lies
The land of the different mind,
Not honey in the brook,
None of the grass you dreamed.
Foresee water on fire,
And notches in a cloud;
Expect noise from a rock,
And faces falling apart.
The pathway underfoot,
Heaving its dust, will cross
A poisonous expanse
Where light knocks down the trees,
And whatever spells you took
Before, you will take anew
From the clack in the high wind.
Nothing will be at ease,
Nothing at peace, but you.

"Tan Ta Ra, Cries Mars . . ."

—Thomas Weelkes

"Clang!" goes the high-framed, feather-tufted gong. The mace
And halberd, jostled together, ring on the cobblestones,
While straight with the horde, blue flies and pieces of wings
Sail to the war. Owl's egg in mouth, the prophet sings
Glory from thumb-stirred entrails, glory from eagle-stains
And smoke, holding a cup of moly to his face.

"Blat!" go the thin-stemmed silver horns. High-tail and
        horse-behind,
Prouder than bustles, rise in the streets to prank
And fidget with the air. See, plumes at their ears,
The unicorns stumble—the ram-horned bugbears,
And the spears, all brassily crested, rank on jack-straw rank,
And the phalanx of bellies, and the rusty, bellying wind.

"Tan Ta Ra!" cries Mars, last in the callithumpian line
Where midgets, riding on dogs, squeak like his chariot wheels
And weep. Ta Ra to his majesty's knotted thighs and fists!
The knuckle-browed, crotch-guarded master of hosts,
The raggedy-hafted Mars goes forth, with stars on his heels,
To battle, twitching our dust behind him like a gown.

Spring Song

O marvelous, our brave delight,
The sun stands in its hole,
And a warrior with a crocus wreath
Goes dancing for his soul,
Trailed closely by a harridan
Leading a milky cow.
Sigh, sigh for our lady,
The Mother of Fragments, now.

Delicate, on their hands and knees
Come Some from upper floors,
Leaping like hoppers, clocks, and toads
To celebrate all fours,
And twelve pocked maidens behind masks
Sing "Cuckolds All A-row."
Sigh, sigh for our lady,
The Mother of Fragments, now.

"I find no darkness in my head,
Alas," cries Bumbling Bill;
"O shake hands with the unenjoyed,"
Says lofty Mirabel.
"Simmer," sings the nightingale;
"Hokum," says the crow.
Sigh, sigh for our lady,
The Mother of Fragments, now.

"I dreamed that I was dead and gone,
Thank God," says Aunty Ann;
"Winter is over! Fold the beds,
And booze," cries Everyman.
"Bees," remarks the lily fly;

"Birdies," says the sow.
Sigh, sigh for our lady,
The Mother of Fragments, now.

O marvelous, O marvelous,
The widow of the weeds
Remembers feather, sun, and coast,
And plaits her bun with seeds,
And all the couriers of flesh
Snaffle themselves anew.
Sigh, sigh for our lady,
The Mother of Fragments, now.

The Feast

Maimed and enormous in the air,
The bird fell down to us and died.
Its eyelids were like cleats of fire,
And fire was pouring from its side.

Beneath the forest and the ash
We stood and watched it. Beak to breast,
It floundered like a dying fish,
Beating its wings upon the dust.

What vague imbalance in our hearts
Leaned us together then? The frost
Came feathered from a sky of quartz;
Huge winter was our holy ghost.

O for light's sake, we turned to see
Waterglass forming on a stone;
A hag laughed under every tree;
The trees came slowly toppling down,

And all of the staring eyes were false.
Our jaws unhinged themselves, grew great,
And then we knelt like animals
To the body of this death, and ate.

The Man from the Top of the Mind

From immaculate construction to half death,
See him: the light bulb screwed into his head,
The vacuum tube of his sex, the electric eye.
What lifts his foot? What does he do for breath?

His nickel steel, oily from neck to wrist,
Glistens as though by sunlight where he stands.
Nerves bought by the inch and muscles on a wheel
Spring in the triple-jointed hooks of his hands.

As plug to socket, or flange along a beam,
Two become one; yet what is he to us?
We cry, "Come, marry the bottom of our minds.
Grant us the strength of your impervium."

But clad in a seamless skin, he turns aside
To do the tricks ordained by his transistors—
His face impassive, his arms raised from the dead,
His switch thrown one way into animus.

Reach for him now, and he will flicker with light,
Divide preposterous numbers by unknowns,
Bump through our mazes like a genius rat,
Or trace his concentric echoes to the moon.

Then, though we beg him, "Love us, hold us fast,"
He will stalk out of focus in the air,
Make gestures in an elemental mist,
And falter there—as we will falter here

When the automaton pretends to dream
And turns in rage upon our horrible shapes—
Those nightmares, trailing shreds of his netherworld,
Who must be slaughtered backward into time.

Murder Mystery

After the murder, like parades of Fools,
The bungling supernumeraries come,
Sniffing at footprints, looking under rugs,
Clasping the dead man with prehensile tools.
Lens against nose, false beard down to his knees,
The Hawkshaw enters, hoists his bag of tricks,
And passes out suspicion like lemonade:
"Where were you when the victim—" "In my room."
"Didn't you ask him whether—" "Double locks."
"Who switched the glasses on the—" "Crippled legs."
"Why were the ballroom curtains—" "Mad for years."
Then, tripping on clues, they wander through the house,
And search each other, frighten themselves with guns,
Ransack the kitchen and the sherry bins,
And dance in the bushes with the cats and dogs.

"Where is he?" says the Captain. "Nobody cares."
"We did it!" scream the butler and the maid.
"I did it too!" the jolly doctor cries.
And all join in—detective, counterfoil,
Ingénue, hero, and the family ghosts—
And, flapping like tongues, the trapdoors babble guilt,
The window-boxes, closets understairs,
Whatnots and chandeliers, grandfather clocks,
The sealed-up attic with its litter of bones—
All of them shake, and pour their secrets out.
And the happy party, bearing aloft the dead,
Handcuffed and drunk, go singing toward the jail;
Stage-hands roll up their sleeves, fold up the lawn,
Dismantle the hedges and the flowerbed,
Then follow, hauling the mansion, to confess.

Meanwhile, in another place—their figures cold,
Both turned to shadows by a single pain,
Bloodless together—the killer and the slain
Have kissed each other in the wilderness,
Touching soft hands and staring at the world.

Memento Mori

In my list of choices, death had not appeared.
The forest in my head, the scrambling words,
The stars and motes behind my eyes grew fierce
And fearsome before sleep. But none were black.
None loomed. In the woods were only birds to be feared;
In words, their loss; in stars, their merciless swords.
By the praise of my flesh, I could always pierce,
With clean ferocity, sleep's cul-de-sac.

I moved through the flaking air and had my say.
Time held its mirrors to my face: I looked,
And nose to nose, I stared my image down.
The rout of cretinous horrors in the night
Had left me cold but steady in my day.
What if the light was huge and steep? I knocked
Out of pride against the sun and dune
To make them speak. They did. I took no fright.

Angels and ashes seemed the freaks of age.
"Bring out your dead," I cried, and cocked my eye
To see the hillocks and the loam-beds stir.
Earth held. No bone broke out. No head of death
Sprang like a comet from the world at large,
Trailing its dark. "Poets refuse to die,"
I wrote on stone. Yet now, O God in Thy blur,
Who is it stuffs this murdering dust in my breath?

Lullaby Through the Side of the Mouth

Goodnight, unlucky three. Mice at a feast
Go nibbling the grain away; the wrens
Fluff one another in the hollow post;
And moths are knuckling at the windowpanes.

O pray to the wall, pray to the billypan,
Render all praise to footboards and the sheets,
Call up the spiral mattress if you can:
But see, at your eyes, the counterclockwise lights.

Now you must sacrifice—first, to the dark,
Next, to the crippled underhalf of the mind—
Your faces, hearts, whatever does good work,
Before you come to the burrows at wit's end.

Once more, the holes lie open into dreams:
In one, a hairless tail; in one, a quill;
And, in a third, antennae with soft plumes.
Now put them on, dear Lust, my Love, poor Will.

My forefeet lift each kernel like a cup;
May beak and claw touch heaven under wings;
May the dust-flecked moth find every window up.
But those are joys. You will not dream such things.

The First Word

There had been sounds before: the trumpeting snout,
The crackling of the earth.
The trees had spoken for a million years;
Water had fallen; the great bees, gesturing,
Droned in their hollows, crying what was sweet.
Deep in his cave, he heard them; and his throat
Clouded with shapes and storms.
What could he do, whose tongue was but a thing?

Was it death-noise first? Or the would-be thunderer,
Man-become weather, shouting at the sky?
Or naked and hungry, mad, nibbling at fur,
The one who heard the Others growl as they bled,
And dreamed his terrible name?
Or did his fingers bring such bitterness
From world to lip
He cried aloud to see them come again?

The sunlight blazed outside, purple and green
On the stones and fern-leaves. Did he call it *day*?
No, but he raised his eyes.
The roof of his mouth was burning like the sun;
The water beneath his tongue had run away,
And Another stood at the entrance like a god.
A voice stirred in the wilderness of his head.
Was it *yes* or *no*? Was it *you* or *me* he said?

from *The Nesting Ground*

(1963)

After Consulting My Yellow Pages

All went well today in the barbers' college:
The razor handles pointed gracefully outward,
The clippers were singing like locusts. And far away
On the fox farms, the red and silver sun brushed lightly
Tail after tail. Happily, the surveyors
Measured the downhill pasture through a theodolite,
Untroubled by birchtrees. The makers of fraternal regalia
Conceived a new star-burst, and the parakeet
In the green bird hospital was coaxed out of danger.
Business came flying out of the horse-meat market,
And under the skillful world, the conduits groped
Forward, heavy with wires, to branch at the lake.
Fish brokers prodded salmon on the walloping dock.
The manifold continuous forms and the luminous
        products
Emerged, endlessly shining, while the cooling towers
Poured water over themselves like elephants.
Busily the deft hands of the locksmith and wig-maker
In basement and loft, in the magnifying light,
Turned at their labors. The universal joints,
Hose-couplings, elastic hosiery, shingles and shakes,
The well-beloved escrow companies, the
        heat-exchangers,
Bead-stringers, makers of disappearing beds,
The air-compressors randy with oxygen—
All sprang, remarkably, out of the swinging doors.

And where were you? What did you do today?

Diary

At Monday dawn, I climbed into my skin
And went to see the money. There were the shills:
I conned them—oh, the coins fell out of their mouths,
And paint peeled from the walls like dollar bills.
Below their money-belts, I did them in.

All day Tuesday, grand in my underwear,
I shopped for the world, bought basements and airplanes,
Bargained for corners and pedestrians
And, when I'd marketed the elms away,
Swiped from the water, stole down to the stones.

Suddenly Wednesday offered me my shirt,
Trousers, and shoes. I put them on to dream
Of the one-way stairway and the skittering cloud,
Of the dangerous, footsore crossing at the heart
Where trees, rivers, and stones reach for the dead.

And the next day meant the encircling overcoat
Wherein I sweltered, woolly as a ram:
From butt to swivel, I hoofed it on the loam,
Exacting tribute from the flock in the grass.
My look passed through the werewolf to the lamb.

Friday shied backwards, pulling off my clothes:
The overcoat fell open like a throat;
Shirt-tail and shoe went spidery as a thought,
And covetous drawers whipped knee-deep in a knot.
My skin in a spiral tapered into gold.

And it was naked Saturday for love
Again: the graft grew milky at a kiss.
I lay on the week with money, lust, and vapor,
Megalomania, fear, the tearing-off,
And love in a coil. On Sunday, I wrote this.

Closing Time

At midnight, flaking down like chromium
Inside the tavern, light slips off the bar
And tumbles in our laps. The tumbler falling
Off the edge of the table goes to pieces
As quick as mercury around our shoes.
Goodnight to shuffleboard and counter-check.
The last ball-bearing pins its magnet down
And sinks into a socket like the moon.

Over the rings around our eyes, the clock
Says time to decipher wives, husbands, and cars
On keychains swinging under bleary light.
Goodnight to folding friends on the parking lot
As parallel as windows in a wallet.
Lined up like empties on the curb, goodnight
To all who make the far side of the street,
Their eyelids pressed as tight as bottlecaps.

Goodnight to those with jacks as openers,
Those whose half-cases chill their pelvises,
And those with nothing on tap all day tomorrow
Who wind up sleeping somewhere cold as stars,
Who make the stairs and landings, but not doors,
Those in the tubs, or hung on banisters,
Those with incinerators in their arms,
Whose mouths lie open for another one.

Goodnight to drivers driven by themselves
To curve through light years at the straightaway.
Goodnight to cloverleaf and yellow-streak,
To all those leading sheriff's deputies
Over soft shoulders into power-poles,
The red-in-the-face whose teeth hang down by nerves,
The far-afield, the breakers of new ground
Who cartwheel out of sight, end over end.

A Guide to Dungeness Spit

Out of wild roses down from the switching road between
    pools
We step to an arm of land washed from the sea.
On the windward shore
The combers come from the strait, from narrows and shoals
Far below sight. To leeward, floating on trees
In a blue cove, the cormorants
Stretch to a point above us, their wings held out like
    skysails.
Where shall we walk? First, put your prints to the sea,
Fill them, and pause there:
Five miles to the lighthouse, curved yellow-and-grey
    miles
Tossed among kelp, abandoned with bleaching rooftrees,
Past reaches and currents;
And we must go afoot at a time when the tide is heeling.
Those whistling overhead are Canada geese;
Some on the waves are loons,
And more on the sand are pipers. There, Bonaparte's gulls
Settle a single perch. Those are sponges.
Those are the ends of bones.
If we cross to the inner shore, the grebes and goldeneyes
Rear themselves and plunge through the still surface,
Fishing below the dunes
And rising alarmed, higher than waves. Those are
    cockleshells.
And these are the dead. I said we would come to these.
Stoop to the stones.
Overturn one: the grey-and-white, inch-long crabs come
    pulsing
And clambering from their hollows, tiptoeing sideways.
They lift their pincers
To defend the dark. Let us step this way. Follow me closely

Past snowy plovers bustling among sand-fleas.
The air grows dense.
You must decide now whether we shall walk for miles and
    miles
And whether all birds are the young of other creatures
Or their own young ones,
Or simply their old selves because they die. One falls,
And the others touch him webfoot or with claws,
Treading him for the ocean.
This is called sanctuary. Those are feathers and scales.
We both go into mist, and it hooks behind us.
Those are foghorns.
Wait, and the bird on the high root is a snowy owl
Facing the sea. Its flashing yellow eyes
Turn past us and return;
And turning from the calm shore to the breakers, utterly
    still,
They lead us by the bay and through the shallows,
Buoy us into the wind.
Those are tears. Those are called houses, and those are
    people.
Here is a stairway past the whites of our eyes.
All our distance
Has ended in the light. We climb to the light in spirals,
And look, between us we have come all the way,
And it never ends
In the ocean, the spit and image of our guided travels.
Those are called ships. We are called lovers.
There lie the mountains.

The Nesting Ground

Piping sharp as a reed,
The small bird stood its ground
Twenty feet from ours.
From the shore, another answered
(The piercing double note
Meant killdeer and killdeer)
And skimmed over the sand,
Over the sparse grass,
Lit, then scurried away,
Flopping, crooking its wing
To flash a jagged streak
And the amber of its back.

When the first bird moved a foot
And struck out at the air,
Two chicks leaped after it,
Their plain heads clear as day.
We walked straight to the spot,
Needing to stir what we love,
Knelt down and found nothing,
Not even when we stared
Each checkered, pebbly stalk
Into its own semblance.
We flattened disbelief
With the four palms of our hands.

But the grown birds broke themselves,
Crippled their cries and wings
So near us, we stood up
To follow their sacrifice
That tempts the nails of creatures
Who, needing flight, forget
Whatever they might have caught

By standing still instead.
We kept on walking, led
By pretended injuries,
Till we were far away,
Then turned, as the birds turned
To sail back to the source
Where we had touched our knees,
And saw through our strongest glass
The young spring out of cover,
Piping one death was over.

Homage

When broken laughter broke
From the edge of a bough
I turned, and a buzzing went
Bushes and yards away
Like a shot and disappeared,
Then quick came humming back
To hang like a red hook
First of all in the air
Embedded in a blur,
Then instantly nowhere.
I glanced from marsh to creek,
To the arches of my eyes
And found flush in the sun
The striking hummingbird
Whirring and chortling down
Faster than I could follow
Within a foot of my ear
Vanishing there and there
Only to reappear
Forty feet aloft,
Unsteady and permanent,
Transfixed, then gone again
To slant straight at my head
But missing, rocketing by.
A streak of redness left
Behind it like a stroke
Bent me down in half,
Bowing me toward its mate
As drab as a burnt leaf
Perched silent at my elbow.

Séance for Two Hands

When all the shades could spell
On slates as though at school
Or rap on the wall,
Life was doing well.
Out of the cracks in marble,
From under the lifted table
Came the shape of the soul:
The wind in a shirt-tail,
A fish in a white veil,
The moon behind an owl.
Though put to bed with a shovel
The body like a wheel
Rose from its rut at will
Nor kept the spirit level.

But the dead no longer press
Against the looking-glass.
They have gone out of the gauze,
Away from the feet of yews;
Their lips no longer pause
At the edges of lilies.
Disenthralled from cats' eyes,
Battered from the cows,
Dropped from the breasts of crows,
Driven from the flies,
The ghosts of the latter days
Of the soul's progress
Needle a point in space.
Death alone haunts our house.

The Emergency Maker

"Still alive—" the message ran,
Tapped on a broken rail—
"The air is somewhere else, the shaft
Is blacker than the coal.
Lower a light and break the rock
That plugged this bloody hole."
But I, who had tossed the dynamite,
Had better things to do
Than juggle stones from here to there
Or bring the dark to day.
Go shovel yourself and hold your nose:
The diggers have to die.

"We'll starve in a week—" the radio said,
Fading in salty weather—
"We've eaten kelp and canvas shoes,
Played at father and mother,
And now we've run out of things to do
To seaweed and each other."
But I, who had drained their compass oil,
Had better fish to fry
Than those I'd caught in a wet canoe
Or over my father's knee.
Go down to the sea and drink your fill:
The lubbers have to die.

"For God's sake—" said the heliograph
High on the mountaintop—
"We're frozen quick on a narrow ledge:
If you want us down, come up.
The avalanche slopes above our heads
Like a nose over a lip."
But I, who had cut their ropes in half,

Gone tumbling down the scree,
Stuffed the crevasse with edelweiss,
And pointed the wrong way,
Said *Pull up your boots and take the air:*
We climbers have to die.

Free Passage

Come away, my sea-lane baggage,
For a crack at the sky.
Come with me in an armlock over the ocean, my china
     breakage,
We shall go everywhere in a day, grant liberty, squeak, and
     never die.

From docks to lavender palaces,
Oh what comings and goings, my rattan May basket!
Adored as we fall through tissue-paper, through balconies,
     fountains, and trellises,
We shall be borne up like desserts in cream, stuffed like a
     brisket,

And spun in the air like platters.
At concerts, we shall arrive in all three aisles at once, be
     lionized in jungles, horsed at the seaside.
Chairmen on tiptoe and the giddy, sidelong doctors
Will toast us and be irrevocably toasted.

I have initialed everything, bought floating flashlights,
Filled my binocular flasks with the hottest chutney.
Bye, Mommy! Bye, Daddy! Bye, Sissy! Bye-bye, Fatso!
I'm salting off on the briny with my candy.

Oh my snifter, my tumble-rick, sweet crank of the stars,
My banjo-bottomed, fretful girl,
Tear off those swatches of silk, your hems and haws, and
     coil them up like streamers—
Get set to toss them over the bounding rail.

Sal volatile! Coral uplift! Oh my pink receiver! Freely I
    swear
Our tanglefoot Rosicrucian wedding on a gangplank,
    among the hoots and the spouting fireboats,
Above flashbulbs, fish-heads, and the drowning divers,
Will be as immortal as rats.

The Calculation

A man six feet tall stands on a curb, facing a light
suspended fifteen feet above the middle of a street
thirty feet wide. He begins to walk along the curb
at five m.p.h. After he has been walking for ten
seconds, at what rate is the length of his shadow
increasing?
　　　　　　　—a problem given by my calculus instructor,
　　　　　　　　　　　　　　　　Penn State, 1946

Facing a streetlight under batty moths
And June bugs ratcheting like broken clock-springs,
I stand, for the sake of a problem, on the curb—
Neither in grass nor gutter—while those wings
Switch down the light and patch my undershirt.

I turn half-right. My shadow cuts a hedge,
Climbs through a rhododendron to a porch,
And nods on a windowsill. How far it goes
I leave to burglars and Pythagoras.
Into the slanting glare I slant my watch,

Then walk five miles per hour, my shoes on edge
In a practiced shuffle past the sewer grid
Over the gold no-parking-or-pausing zones
And into the clear—five seconds—into dirt,
Then over a sawhorse studded with lanterns,

And at the tenth I stiffen like a stump
Whose lopped head ripples with concentric figures,
Note the location of my other head
In a garden, but keep trundling forward,
Ignoring *Doppelgängers* from moon and lawn-lamp,

My eyes alert now, leveling my feet,
Seeing my shadow sweeping like a scythe

Across the stalks of daisies, barking trees,
And scraping up the blistered weatherboard
To the eaves of houses, scaling the rough shingles.

At fifteen seconds, in a vacant lot,
My head lies on a board. I count it off.
I think back to the garden, and I guess,
Instructor, after fifteen years of sweat,
It was increasing five feet plus per second.

At the start, I could have fallen, turned around,
Or crossed to the very center of confusion,
My shadow like a manhole, no one's length,
Or the bulb itself been broken with a shot,
And all my reckoning have gone unreckoned.

But I was late because my shadow was
Pointing toward nothing like the cess of light,
Sir, and bearing your cold hypotenuse—
That cutter of corners, jaywalker of angles—
On top of my head, I walked the rest of the night.

Elegy for Simon Corl, Botanist

With wildflowers bedded in his mind,
My blind great-uncle wrote a book.
His lips and beard were berry-stained,
Wrist broken like a shepherd's crook.

His door leaned open to the flies,
And May, like tendrils, wandered in.
The earth rose gently to his knees;
The clouds moved closer than his skin.

Sun against ear, he heard the slight
Stamen and pistil touch for days,
Felt pollen cast aslant like light
Into the shadows of his eyes.

When autumn stalked the leaves, he curled;
His fingers ripened like the sky;
His ink ran to a single word,
And the straight margin went awry.

When frost lay bristling on the weeds,
He smoothed it with a yellow thumb,
Followed his white cane to the woods
Between the saxifrage and thyme,

And heard the hornets crack like ice,
Felt worms arch backward in the snow;
And while the mites died under moss,
The clean scar sang across his brow.

Offertory

Ready to leave for work, I look around
To check windows and switches: in the sink,
A pool of coffee poured from the last cup
Gleams near the drain; the ring in the bath
At its own level holds my body up;
And crumpled on the bed, blankets like sheep
Crouch where the ram came, reeling, from his dip.
So many rituals: two cups for the gods
Of the left and right temple, the grounds gone
Where all libations go; on porcelain,
My yesterday in an upright, shrinking lather;
Dial down and ticking under the pillow-slip,
Two sheets to the wind hauled back from sleep—
I leave these for the maker of light whose rain
On the alarming morning fell again.

45

Plumage

Beside a bush, the pheasant on one foot
Is standing motionless, green head erect,
Bronze belly feathers washing into grass.
He stares to know me. Staring back, I see
Each wing-bar tasselled like a shock of wheat,
The tail grained edgewise, shoulders flaking white,
His buff flank strewn with black, a scarlet cheek
Cupped to an eye-spot like a flowerhead.

But where? He falls to pieces in my eye—
To flinders, flaws of intersecting light
Where dust and the veins of leaves are cancelled out,
Cross-hatched and baffled at the edge of sight—
And pours all distance forward through a speck
Till stalk and stick, spikelet and ripe seed
Go hedging back as one in the hedgerow.
Too carelessly, I take another breath.

Out of the shadows, booming, rocketing,
Shaking direction, breaking left and right,
The pheasant clappers upward, leaves behind
Nothing in amber, neither claw nor strut,
No gaping side, no parcel of a wing
Clipped off by birdshot as a proof of death.
Flashing across a gulley up the wind,
Again, he drops to pieces in the sun.

Once upon a Picnic Ground

Once upon a picnic ground
Our love was in the bag,
And bread and butter by the pound
Was easily ours to beg.
The nancy boys and gutter girls
Fell over themselves to fetch
The hard-boiled eggs and carrot curls
We needed in the clutch.

And twice upon a picnic ground
Our love lay on the table.
Whenever we passed our plates around,
It gave us heaps of trouble:
Up from our pot of boston beans
Molasses overflowed
And, sticking against our hotdog buns,
Undid the work of God.

When these events were stuffed, we found
Our bag was full of shells,
And ginger bears, without a sound,
Came in their hairy shawls
Through sweet incinerator smoke—
Their muzzles caked with crumbs—
To budge us out of the way and make
A bed for stumblebums.

Now robber jays and pheasant hens
Cry from the hemlock tree
Above the streaming garbagecans
For my lost love and me.
Their craws are full of lightning-bugs;
Their molting feathers cross
On bottles, bags, and bearskin rugs,
And the enduring grass.

No Sale

Shushing their ankle dogs,
The women behind doors
In curlers, saying No,
All wore their lipstick thin,
Waited till I would go,
Then latched themselves back in.

At the corner in his car
The siding salesman said,
"A high-class canvasser
Tickles them through the screen.
Look them straight in the chest.
Quit telling the truth."

And after pounding weeks
Through showers and heat-waves
At a glance I knew the worst
Weatherboards and shakes
Or paint like blistered heels.
By hundreds of yards and stairs

I talked to all the wives
Who leaned on shaky walls.
I said an engineer
Was waiting at their pleasure
To insulate their sides,
To hold their windows up.

I slummed them, saying floors
Would warp them out of place.
Get ready to play house
Like cards, as serious
As mothers playing trumps.
What else can save your face?

I said a house needs skin
Thicker than powder-base
To stop the sagging, keep
The plaster in its cast,
Packed around bones for years.
But nothing turned their heads.

Swindled by someone else,
They sat in curls all day,
Waiting to be let down,
Waiting to fall straight
And stringy at midnight.
So I went straight, and quit.

The Breathing Lesson

"Sensations of smell are relatively homogeneous
and untranslatable into the form of language.
Nobody can enlarge upon an odor."
—Oscar W. Firkins

Around the compass, soap-flakes and burnt corn,
A swamp, the acid cracked from boiling oil,
Sulfur dioxide, plumage of soft coal,
The yellow wreckage of Lake Michigan—
The unpredictable first breath of a day
Where I grew up depended on the wind.

My life would turn tail like a weathervane
And find attention wrung out on the line,
My breath in dollops, dead frogs in the throat,
The drill in the forehead, branches of membrane
Flocking with soot, or the unhallowed dregs
Of the lake come lapping up like burlap dogs.

Led by the nose around the pit of self
In all directions, I was washerwoman,
The dying year-god, infidel at the gate,
The egg of the world, machine-man, rancid goat.
But if the wind was veering, backing off,
They choked themselves on metamorphosis.

O Lux, Mazola, Wolf Lake, Standard Oil,
O city dump, O docks of Bethlehem—
Though a mind, run through its middle, can't forget
What creatures roamed its baffling passages,
In the dead calm of morning once, I rose
Breathless without your help, and walked away.

The Satirists

With verminous ringlets leaping on their wigs,
They staggered through the city, stuttering rage
At a world pulled inside out by hypocrites.
Lace to their elbows, elbows steeped in swill,
The carpet-knights answered like Latin-mongers;
The acrobats and prigs guffawed in the dark
To praise, like cats, the tickling end of the quill.

Oh indignation lit their cheeks like chilblains,
And while their gouty great-toes pulsed on the stones,
Gin Lane flocked out to chorus, "Up smocks all!"
Ambition rolled with Simony in the streets
Where life lay squeezed into its opposites.
"Reform!" they shouted, but their voices wheezed
Like drainpipes through an ever-thickening phlegm.
"Blindmen!" they cried, and jumped out of their shoes,
But still the pock-faced pimps gnawed at the moon.

Toasting themselves in black and yellow bile,
They turned splenetic wisdom to the wall,
Weeping for Donkeys and the City of Christ
Or country pleasures beaten into holes.
Those great, blood-let, exacerbated men—
Foredoomed to choke like thieves on their own
        tongues—
All muttered, "Cover your hearts and trim them close,"
While they lurched home to cork anonymous wives.

Advice to the Orchestra

Start like pieces of string:
Lank homeliness attached, maybe, to nothing.
Then oh! my harpies, brush over the rows and thrust
Music like brooms under their chairs, rouse out the cats, the
      purses, and the dust.
Make them all leap up—the ophthalmic trance-breakers, the
      doggers, midge-killers, all the pie-faced gawkies and
      their crumbs.
Give them music to break their glasses, to knock their eyelids
      up like hatbrims.

When they run, follow them out of doors, out of windows,
Assault their tails with chorts and tootles, oompahs and
      glissandos.
Snare them. Give them no hiding places. Let them be draked
      in the reeds.
Slide after them into dumps and suburbs, over trembling
      hairpin roads,
Across channels and bays to the tilted islands where water
      whirls on edge.
Spiral through tunnels, over the baffling rocks and the spokes
      of forests, to the last desperate wheelprint, committing
      outrage.

Oh my outlandish ones,
Offer yourselves through the mold on brass, through skins
      and bones.
Your music must consume its instruments
Or die lost in the elbow-joints and valves, in snaggle and
      crook, ratchet and pinchbeck, in the folded winds.
Let the boom come. Send up the burning brows,
The white domes of your echoes.

Stand in the pit. Strike the sides of your death. Let spherical thunder
Rise from gravel-throated, unharmonious earth, the stricken center,
Beyond air fringed like a curtain, through the cabbage leaves and angels of the moon,
The mercurial archangels,—rise to untune
The principalities and powers, the squash of the sun, virtues and jovial dominations, the saturnine thrones, calliope-pumping cherubim and seraphim with their heads ablaze
Against the old gods' mobile, eccentric knees.

Out for a Night

It was No, no, no, practicing at a chair,
And No at the wall, and one for the fireplace,
And down the stairs it was No over the railing,
And two for the dirt, and three Noes for the air,

And four in a row rapidly over the bar,
Becoming Maybe, Maybe, from spittoon to mirror,
It was shrugging cheeks on one face after another,
And Perhaps and So-So at both ends of a cigar,

Five, and it was Yes as a matter of fact
Who said it wasn't all the way down the bottle,
It was Hell Yes over and lightly underfoot,
And tongue like a welcome mat for the bartender,

And Yes in the teeth, Yes like a cracked whistle,
And one for you, and two for the rest of us,
Indeed, Indeed, the chair got up on the table,
And Yes got up on the chair and kissed the light

And the light burned, and Yes fell out of the chair,
And the chair slid off the table, and it was Maybe
All over the floor, tilted, it was squat,
And plunge to the rear, and smack lips like a baby,

It was five for the fingers Absolutely,
Four in the corners, it was three for the show,
And two descending eyebrows to make a ceiling,
And No to the knees and chin, and one Goodbye.

Every Good Boy Does Fine

I practiced my cornet in a cold garage
Where I could blast it till the oil in drums
Boomed back; tossed free-throws till I couldn't move my
    thumbs;
Sprinted through tires, tackling a headless dummy.

In my first contest, playing a wobbly solo,
I blew up in the coda, alone on stage,
And twisting like my hand-tied necktie, saw the judge
Letting my silence dwindle down his scale.

At my first basketball game, gangling away from home
A hundred miles by bus to a dressing room,
Under the showering voice of the coach, I stood in a towel,
Having forgotten shoes, socks, uniform.

In my first football game, the first play under the lights
I intercepted a pass. For seventy yards, I ran
Through music and squeals, surging, lifting my cleats,
Only to be brought down by the safety man.

I took my second chances with less care, but in dreams
I saw the bald judge slumped in the front row,
The coach and team at the doorway, the safety man
Galloping loud at my heels. They watch me now.

You who have always horned your way through passages,
Sat safe on the bench while some came naked to court,
Slipped out of arms to win in the long run,
Consider this poem a failure, sprawling flat on a page.

That Old Gang of Mine

"Warden, I thank you." "Not at all." He bowed.
With my dress cane, I hit him on the head.

"A stirring evening, Officer." The guard
Blinked at my spinning watch-chain. Then he snored.

"Come out, good thieves," I whispered to the walls,
And heard the fine teeth mousing in the cells.

Sliding the key-ring under the cold bars,
I tiptoed down the hall and out of doors.

The first explosion coughed the windows out;
The second made stones generous to a fault;

The third threw up the prison, clapped its wings,
Squinted the lights, and pierced the sirens' lungs.

Over the rubble in their shredded suits,
Out of the tangle of bent license plates,

Through the dim ruckus between dust and guns,
Came my key men, the unlocked skeletons,

Bumping their knobby knees against the rocks
That once stood tall as hell to shepherd crooks.

"Run for our lives!" I whispered. "First comes grass,
Then shrubs, then trees, then water, and then grace."

Oscar the Bounder ripped his jacket off
And vaulted toward the deep night in the buff.

Phineas the Mouthpiece staggered, his eyes shut,
And hawked to break the thick years in his throat.

Sylvester the One-man Sack-race, self-possessed,
Stalked through the brambles, lofty as a post.

Esau the Actor, two feet, four feet, none,
Rose past the willows, flickered, and was gone.

Then out of the heap, the unpacked bloodhounds came
Groggy but eager, snuffling the old game.

Fit to be tied behind them, stumbling guards
Saw their long leashes snarling into braids

As we went crosspath, taking to our heels
In five directions, tireless through the hills.

At dawn, across the water, over the dunes,
Past the bleak alders and the bleaker downs,

Over the thorn scrub like *cheval-de-frise,*
I went to meet them, purple with their praise,

And as we leaped and crowed in a shower of cash,
We danced a ring around the burning bush.

A Day in the City

Dismounting from stools and benches, pouring through bars,
Let's do the day up brown,
Knock it back like a short drink, get off our trolley,
Put our foot downtown.

There, cutting the sun in half with our eyelids,
Sinister with love,
We shall wait till those feet, swollen to thousands on the
    pavement,
Are aching to move.

Then from the joints at our knees, the crooks at our elbows,
From all the hugging sides,
Through the calves and hams, the perpendicular marches
Will drill us into squads.

Rising from cornerstones, cripples with bristling pencils
Will jam on their caps
And join us—the floorwalkers and shoplifters, gulls and
    barkers,
The blindmen in their cups,

And the chirruping children, the sailors and loaded Indians,
Fur-bearing stylish stouts,
All thronging from broken curb to curb and up the
    lamp-posts,
Onto ledges like goats.

And the city is ours. See, the bridges all give up, the arcades
Rattle their silver shops,
Buildings chip in, the sidewalks roll over like dogs, hotels
Chime their fire-escapes.

Here on a glittering carpet of plate glass go dancing
Till leggings and bandages
Trail us like trains round the fountain to the plaza, till our
    faces
Leap from our jaws,

And our sleeves roll back to the trombones and armbands,
And, shooting the mailchutes,
We stand in circles on every floor, shaking our palms,
Flagging our bedsheets.

We shall trump up a total noise, a silence battered
Like rams in the air.
Let the sewers hoot, all risers drop their treads
To the wrenched foot of the stair.

Then quietly, left and right, with our bandoliers
Crossed on our blouses,
We shall drift away through the empty business-ends of the
    streets
To go back to pieces,

While the city lets out the fiery-red, grumbling water-wagons
To lay the dust,
And sends toward our houses, through every alley,
The huge, defaced,

Skulking, familiar, handle-breaking, off-key garbageman
Who had been killed,
But who now heaps under the raised lids, our old lives
Before they are cold.

On Seeing an X-Ray of My Head

Now face to face, hard head, old nodder and shaker,
While we still have ears,
Accept my congratulations: you survived
My headlong blunders
As, night by night, my knuckles beat at your brow
More often than at doors,
Yet you were pampered, waved from the end of your
    stick
Like a bird in feathers,
Wrapped in towels, whistled and night-capped,
And pressed into pillows.
I see by this, the outline of our concern,
What you will lose
Before too long: the shadowy half of chin
And prodding nose,
Thatchwork of hair, loose tongue, and parting lips,
My look as blank as yours,
And yet, my madcap, catch-all rattlepot,
Nothing but haze
Shows on this picture what we had in mind,
The crannied cauliflower
Ready to boil away at a moment's notice
In a fit of vapors
And leave us holding the bag. Oh my brainpan,
When we start our separate ways
With opaque, immortal fillings clenched in our teeth
Like a bunch of keys,
And when your dome goes rolling into a ditch
And, slack in the jaws,
Stops at a hazard, some unplayable lie,
Accept at your ease
Directly what was yours at one remove:
Light through your eyes,

Air, dust, and water as themselves at last. Keep smiling.
Consider the source.
Go back to the start, old lime-pit, remembering flesh
        and skin,
Your bloody forebears.

Standing Halfway Home

At the last turn in the path, where locust thorns
Halter my sleeve, I suddenly stand still
For no good reason, planting both my shoes.
No other takes its place when my noise ends.
The hush is on. Through the deserted boughs,
Through fireweed, bracken, duff, down to the ground,
The air comes as itself without a sound
And deepens at my knees like waste of breath.

Behind my back lies the end of property;
Ahead, around a corner, a new house.
Barbed wire and aerials cross up and out
To mark the thresholds of man's common sense:
Keep out, keep talking. Doing neither one,
Here, central and inert, I stop my mouth
To reassure all the invisible
For whom my sight and sound were dangerous.

Eyes in the wings of butterflies stare through
The hazel leaves. Frozen beside my foot,
A tawny skink relaxes on its toes.
I shift my weight. The sun bears down the hill,
And overhead, past where an eye can turn,
A hiss of feathers parts the silence now.
At my arm's length a seedy, burr-sized wren,
As if I were a stalk, bursts into song.

The Observer

The woman kneeling by the side of the road
Sketches a porcupine lying dead,
Its tail on pavement, chest on the narrow shoulder.
The waxed face of the moon wears through the sky.
She turns a page and reaches out to touch
The quills left upright on the scruff of its neck.
Rising, she circles, and a car sweeps by:
The trailing wind goes past her, and the dust
Swerves to a standstill, hovers, and falls down.

For an hour, I've waited while the night sank in,
And now she takes her loose windbreaker sleeve
To drag the spiny heap over the gravel
And into the weeds, breaking a foxglove
Against its side as if by accident.

I join her to see the black soles of its paws,
Yellow incisors grinning in profile,
Its pale-tipped jaggers aimed from the dead center.
Thrusting dim lights ahead, another car
Drags its pursuing vacuum down the line.
We hold ourselves against the buffeting,
Then walk toward our house and a level bed;
But on the bank she trips out of one sandal
And, sitting down without it, holds her head.

She knows a porcupine is drawn from its life
Or—like the quills shoved out the other side
Of flesh because the irreversible barbs
Take one way out—takes this way out of death.
I rub her foot. No need to mention love.

Filling Out a Blank

High School Profile-Achievement Form
for D. Wagoner, 1943 . . . Item 8,
Job Preferences: 1) Chemist
2) Stage Magician 3)——

My preference was to be
The shrewd man holding up
A test-tube to the light,
Or the bowing charlatan
Whose inexhaustible hat
Could fill a stage with birds.
Lying beyond that,
Nothing seemed like me.

Imagining the years
In a smock or a frock coat
Where all was black or white,
Idly I set about
To conjure up a man
In a glare, concocting life
Like a rich precipitate
By acid out of base.

What shivered up my sleeve
Was neither rabbit nor gold,
But a whole bag of tricks:
The bubbling of retorts
In sterile corridors,
Explosions and handcuffs,
Time falling through trapdoors
In a great cloud of smoke.

But the third guess leaves me cold:
It made me draw a blank,
A stroke drawn with my pen
Going from left to right
And fading out of ink
As casually as a fact.
It came to this brief line,
This disappearing act.

from *Staying Alive*
(1966)

The Words

Wind, bird, and tree,
Water, grass, and light:
In half of what I write
Roughly or smoothly
Year by impatient year,
The same six words recur.

I have as many floors
As meadows or rivers,
As much still air as wind
And as many cats in mind
As nests in the branches
To put an end to these.

Instead, I take what is:
The light beats on the stones,
And wind over water shines
Like long grass through the trees,
As I set loose, like birds
In a landscape, the old words.

Staying Alive

Staying alive in the woods is a matter of calming down
At first and deciding whether to wait for rescue,
Trusting to others,
Or simply to start walking and walking in one direction
Till you come out—or something happens to stop you.
By far the safer choice
Is to settle down where you are, and try to make a living
Off the land, camping near water, away from shadows.
Eat no white berries;
Spit out all bitterness. Shooting at anything
Means hiking further and further every day
To hunt survivors;
It may be best to learn what you have to learn without a gun,
Not killing but watching birds and animals go
In and out of shelter
At will. Following their example, build for a whole season:
Facing across the wind in your lean-to,
You may feel wilder,
But nothing, not even you, will have to stay in hiding.
If you have no matches, a stick and a fire-bow
Will keep you warmer,
Or the crystal of your watch, filled with water, held up to
	the sun
Will do the same in time. In case of snow
Drifting toward winter,
Don't try to stay awake through the night, afraid of freezing—
The bottom of your mind knows all about zero;
It will turn you over
And shake you till you waken. If you have trouble sleeping
Even in the best of weather, jumping to follow
With eyes strained to their corners
The unidentifiable noises of the night and feeling
Bears and packs of wolves nuzzling your elbow,
Remember the trappers

Who treated them indifferently and were left alone.
If you hurt yourself, no one will comfort you
Or take your temperature,
So stumbling, wading, and climbing are as dangerous as flying.
But if you decide, at last, you must break through
In spite of all danger,
Think of yourself by time and not by distance, counting
Wherever you're going by how long it takes you;
No other measure
Will bring you safe to nightfall. Follow no streams: they run
Under the ground or fall into wilder country.
Remember the stars
And moss when your mind runs into circles. If it should rain
Or the fog should roll the horizon in around you,
Hold still for hours
Or days if you must, or weeks, for seeing is believing
In the wilderness. And if you find a pathway,
Wheel-rut, or fence-wire,
Retrace it left or right: someone knew where he was going
Once upon a time, and you can follow
Hopefully, somewhere,
Just in case. There may even come, on some uncanny evening,
A time when you're warm and dry, well fed, not thirsty,
Uninjured, without fear,
When nothing, either good or bad, is happening.
This is called staying alive. It's temporary.
What occurs after
Is doubtful. You must always be ready for something to come
          bursting
Through the far edge of a clearing, running toward you,
Grinning from ear to ear
And hoarse with welcome. Or something crossing and
          hovering
Overhead, as light as air, like a break in the sky,

Wondering what you are.
Here you are face to face with the problem of recognition.
Having no time to make smoke, too much to say,
You should have a mirror
With a tiny hole in the back for better aiming, for reflecting
Whatever disaster you can think of, to show
The way you suffer.
These body signals have universal meaning: If you are lying
Flat on your back with arms outstretched behind you,
You say you require
Emergency treatment; if you are standing erect and holding
Arms horizontal, you mean you are not ready;
If you hold them over
Your head, you want to be picked up. Three of anything
Is a sign of distress. Afterward, if you see
No ropes, no ladders,
No maps or messages falling, no searchlights or trails blazing,
Then, chances are, you should be prepared to burrow
Deep for a deep winter.

The Fruit of the Tree

With a wall and a ditch between us, I watched the gate-legged dromedary
Creak open from her sleep and come head-first toward me
As I held out three rust-mottled, tough pears, the color of camels.
When I tossed one, she made no move to catch it; whatever they eat
Lies still and can wait: the roots and sticks, the scrag-ends of brambles.

She straddled, dipping her neck; grey lips and lavender tongue,
Which can choose the best of thorns, thrust the pear to her gullet.
Choking, she mouthed it; her ruminating jaw swung up;
Her eyes lashed out. With a groan she crushed it down,
And ecstasy swept her down into the ditch, till her chin

And her pointed, prolonged face sat on the wall. She stared
At me, inventor and founder of pears. I emptied my sack.
She ate them painfully, clumsy with joy, her withers trembling,
Careless of dust on the bitten and dropped halves, ignoring flies,
Losing herself in the pit of her last stomach.

When she gazed at me again, our mouths were both deserted.
I walked away with myself. She watched me disappear,
Then with a rippling trudge went back to her stable
To snort, to browse on hay, to remember my sack forever.
She'd been used to having no pears, but hadn't known it.

Imagine the hostile runners, the biters of burnouses,
Coughers and spitters, whose legs can kick at amazing angles—
Their single humps would carry us willingly over dunes
Through sandstorms and the swirling djinn to the edges of oases
If they, from their waterless, intractable hearts, might stretch
        for pears.

73

House-Hunting

The wind has twisted the roof from an old house
 And thrown it away,
And no one's going to live there anymore.
 It tempts me:
Why not have weather falling in every room?
 Isn't the sky
As easy to keep up as any ceiling?
 Less flat and steady?
Rain is no heavier, soaking heavy heads,
 Than a long party.
Imagine moonlight for a chandelier,
 Sun through the laundry,
The snow on conversation, leaves in the bed,
 Fog in the library,
Or yourself in a bathtub hoping for the best
 As the clouds go by,
Dressing for dinner according to what comes down
 And not how many.
And at night, to sit indoors would be to lose
 Nothing but privacy
As the crossing stars took time to mark their flight
 Over the mind's eye.

The Shooting of John Dillinger Outside the Biograph Theater, July 22, 1934

Chicago ran a fever of a hundred and one that groggy Sunday.
A reporter fried an egg on a sidewalk; the air looked shaky.
And a hundred thousand people were in the lake like shirts in
a laundry.
Why was Johnny lonely?
Not because two dozen solid citizens, heat-struck, had keeled
over backward.
Not because those lawful souls had fallen out of their sockets
and melted.
But because the sun went down like a lump in a furnace or a
bull in the Stockyards.
Where was Johnny headed?
Under the Biograph Theater sign that said, "Our Air is
Refrigerated."
Past seventeen FBI men and four policemen who stood in
doorways and sweated.
Johnny sat down in a cold seat to watch Clark Gable get
electrocuted.
Had Johnny been mistreated?
Yes, but Gable told the D. A. he'd rather fry than be shut up
forever.
Two women sat by Johnny. One looked sweet, one looked like
J. Edgar Hoover.
Polly Hamilton made him feel hot, but Anna Sage made him
shiver.
Was Johnny a good lover?
Yes, but he passed out his share of squeezes and pokes like a
jittery masher
While Agent Purvis sneaked up and down the aisle like an
extra usher,
Trying to make sure they wouldn't slip out till the show was
over.

Was Johnny a fourflusher?
No, not if he knew the game. He got it up or got it back.
But he liked to take snapshots of policemen with his own
    Kodak,
And once in a while he liked to take them with an automatic.
Why was Johnny frantic?
Because he couldn't take a walk or sit down in a movie
Without being afraid he'd run smack into somebody
Who'd point at his rearranged face and holler, "Johnny!"
Was Johnny ugly?
Yes, because Dr. Wilhelm Loeser had given him a new profile
With a baggy jawline and squint eyes and an erased dimple,
With kangaroo-tendon cheekbones and a gigolo's mustache
    that should've been illegal.
Did Johnny love a girl?
Yes, a good-looking, hard-headed Indian named Billie
    Frechette.
He wanted to marry her and lie down and try to get over it,
But she was locked in jail for giving him first-aid and comfort.
Did Johnny feel hurt?
He felt like breaking a bank or jumping over a railing
Into some panicky teller's cage to shout, "Reach for the
    ceiling!"
Or like kicking some vice president in the bum checks and
    smiling.
What was he really doing?
Going up the aisle with the crowd and into the lobby
With Polly saying, "Would *you* do what Clark done?" And
    Johnny saying, "Maybe."
And Anna saying, "If he'd been smart, he'd of acted like Bing
    Crosby."
Did Johnny look flashy?
Yes, his white-on-white shirt and tie were luminous.
His trousers were creased like knives to the tops of his shoes,

And his yellow straw hat came down to his dark glasses.
Was Johnny suspicious?
Yes, and when Agent Purvis signalled with a trembling cigar,
Johnny ducked left and ran out of the theater,
And innocent Polly and squealing Anna were left nowhere.
Was Johnny a fast runner?
No, but he crouched and scurried past a friendly liquor store
Under the coupled arms of double-daters, under awnings,
     under stars,
To the curb at the mouth of an alley. He hunched there.
Was Johnny a thinker?
No, but he was thinking more or less of Billie Frechette
Who was lost in prison for longer than he could possibly wait,
And then it was suddenly too hard to think around a bullet.
Did anyone shoot straight?
Yes, but Mrs. Etta Natalsky fell out from under her picture hat.
Theresa Paulus sprawled on the sidewalk, clutching her left
     foot.
And both of them groaned loud and long under the streetlight.
Did Johnny like that?
No, but he lay down with those strange women, his face in the
     alley,
One shoe off, cinders in his mouth, his eyelids heavy.
When they shouted questions at him, he talked back to
     nobody.
Did Johnny lie easy?
Yes, holding his gun and holding his breath as a last trick,
He waited, but when the Agents came close, his breath
     wouldn't work.
Clark Gable walked his last mile; Johnny ran half a block.
Did he run out of luck?
Yes, before he was cool, they had him spread out on dished-in
     marble
In the Cook County Morgue, surrounded by babbling people

With a crime reporter presiding over the head of the table.
Did Johnny have a soul?
Yes, and it was climbing his slippery wind-pipe like a trapped
    burglar.
It was beating the inside of his ribcage, hollering, "Let me out
    of here!"
Maybe it got out, and maybe it just stayed there.
Was Johnny a money-maker?
Yes, and thousands paid 25¢ to see him, mostly women,
And one said, "I wouldn't have come, except he's a moral
    lesson,"
And another, "I'm disappointed. He feels like a dead man."
Did Johnny have a brain?
Yes, and it always worked best through the worst of dangers,
Through flat-footed hammerlocks, through guarded doors,
    around corners,
But it got taken out in the morgue and sold to some doctors.
Could Johnny take orders?
No, but he stayed in the wicker basket carried by six men
Through the bulging crowd to the hearse and let himself be
    locked in,
And he stayed put as it went driving south in a driving rain.
And he didn't get stolen?
No, not even after his old hard-nosed dad refused to sell
The quick-drawing corpse for $10,000 to somebody in a
    carnival.
He figured he'd let *Johnny* decide how to get to Hell.
Did anyone wish him well?
Yes, half of Indiana camped in the family pasture,
And the minister said, "With luck, he could have been a
    minister."
And up the sleeve of his oversized gray suit, Johnny twitched
    a finger.

78

Does anyone remember?
Everyone still alive. And some dead ones. It was a new kind of
holiday
With hot and cold drinks and hot and cold tears. They planted
him in a cemetery
With three unknown vice presidents, Benjamin Harrison, and
James Whitcomb Riley,
Who never held up anybody.

The Draftsmen, 1945

Given one wall and a roof at a wild angle,
The problem was to find the rest of the house
In Engineering Drawing, to string it along
Its three spread-eagled ninety-degree dimensions
(A line is only a line when it lies flat),
Then trace it up and over, tracking it down
At last to a blunt façade with a shut door.

The whole hot room of us on dunces' stools
Maneuvered compasses and triangles
Over the sliding T-squares and onion skin,
Trying to be on all six sides of a house
At the same time, locking slabs in place
As firmly as the edges of our graves.

We stared at the box like catty-cornered neighbors
Or, losing our perspective, swivelled the earth
Like one-eyed gods till porches spread their wings
And the slant sunlight's isometric waves
Levelled all distance, simply, at a stroke.

And that was that—top, profiles, and front view,
The backside and the rat's collapsible heaven:
Spaces cut out of space like paper dolls
And modelled on a blank interior.

None of us had to draw it inside out,
Sketch in the beds, let smoke through broken windows,
Locate the milkman bleeding in the garden,

Or cross-hatch people running off the paper
Where weather crumpled the uneven corners,

Or knock at the door for any other answers.

The Night of the Sad Women

They are undressing slowly by closed doors,
Unable to find themselves, fading in mirrors
And feeling faint, finding their eyes in time
But seeing, instead, the rooms behind their shoulders

Where nothing is going to work, where photographs
Stand still in frames, arresting other days
When things were turning out. Now turning in,
They are lowering shades and turning off the lights,

But find their fingers lighter than pale linen
At the sinking bedside, seeing their own hands
In front of their faces wavering like gauze,
Then edging away to search in fallen purses.

But they lose touch. In the middle of their rooms
The night begins, the night of the loose threads
Which hang like spiders' lifelines out of seams
To be ravelled to the floor, but not to end.

Water Music for the Progress
of Love in a Life-Raft
down the Sammamish Slough

Slipping at long last from the shore, we wave
        To no one in a house
With a dismantled chimney, a sprung gate,
        And five bare windows,
And begin this excursion under thorny vines
        Trailing like streamers
Over the mainstream, in our inflated life-raft,
        Bluer and yellower
Than the sky and sun which hold the day together.
        My love, upstream,
Be the eyes behind me, saying yes and no.
        I'm manning the short oars
Which must carry us with the current, or without it,
        Six miles to our pasture.
There go the mallards patched with grey and white
        By their tame fathers;
Down from the leaves the kingfishers branching go
        Raucous under the willows
And out of sight; the star-backed salmon are waiting
        For the rain to rise above us;
And the wind is sending our raft like a water spider
        Skimming over the surface.
We begin our lesson here, our slight slow progress,
        Sitting face to face,
Able to touch our hands or soaking feet
        But not to kiss
As long as we must wait at opposite ends,
        Keeping our balance,
Our spirits cold as the Sammamish mud,
        Our tempers rising

Among the drifts like the last of the rainbows rising
          Through the remaining hours
Till the sun goes out. What have I done to us?
          I offer these strands,
These unromantic strains, unable to give
          Such royal accompaniment
As horns on the Thames or bronze bells on the Nile
          Or the pipes of goatmen,
But here, the goats themselves in the dying reeds,
          The ringing cows
And bullocks on the banks, pausing to stare
          At our confluence
Along the awkward passage to the bridge
          Over love's divisions.
Landing at nightfall, letting the air run out
          Of what constrained us,
We fold it together, crossing stem to stern,
          Search for our eyes,
And reach ourselves, in time, to wake again
          This music from silence.

The Poets Agree
to Be Quiet by the Swamp

They hold their hands over their mouths
And stare at the stretch of water.
What can be said has been said before:
Strokes of light like herons' legs in the cattails,
Mud underneath, frogs lying even deeper.
Therefore, the poets may keep quiet.
But the corners of their mouths grin past their hands.
They stick their elbows out into the evening,
Stoop, and begin the ancient croaking.

The Man of the House

My father, looking for trouble, would find it
On his hands and knees by hammering on walls
Between the joists or drilling through baseboards
Or crawling into the attic where insulation
Lay under the leaks like sleeping-bags.

It would be something simple as a rule
To be ingenious for, in overalls;
And he would kneel beside it, pouring sweat
Down his red cheeks, glad of a useful day
With something wrong unknown to the landlord.

At those odd times when everything seemed to work
All right, suspiciously all right like silence
In concrete shelters, he'd test whatever hung
Over our heads: such afternoons meant ladders,
Nails in the mouth, flashing and shaking roofs.

In safety shoes going down basement stairs,
He'd flick his rewired rearrangement of lights
And chase all shadows into the coalbin
Where they could watch him, blinking at his glare.
If shadows hadn't worked, he would have made them.

With hands turning to horn against the stone
He'd think on all fours, hunch as if to drink
If his cold chisel broke the cold foundation
And brought dark water pulsing out of clay.
Wrenching at rows of pipes like his cage-bars,

He made them creak in sockets and give way,
But rammed them back, putting his house in order.
Moonlight or rain, after the evening paper,
His mouth lay open under the perfect plaster
To catch the first sweet drop, but none came down.

85

For the Warming of an Artist's Studio

The previous tenant, running out of business,
Bolted the back door,
Blew out the fuses, sprang the toilet trap,
Unscrewed the hardware,
And didn't leave a trace of his side-kicks—
No cold cashier
Behind the hole in the window saying No,
And no go-getter
Coughing to break the gathering punch-line
At the water-cooler.
Tonight, we'll drink to him. He left the ceiling,
The best part of the floor,
And enough strength in the walls to take the weight
Of an easel's crossbar
On which to float some stock in an enterprise
Also going under
Eventually after going upside-down,
Slantwise and haywire,
But never simply crossing into the red
Like a line in a ledger.
Here goes an artist after a businessman
Not as a panhandler
But, following him through rundown neighborhoods
And making over
The empty premises at the end of his line,
As a silent partner.

Waiting on the Curb

Death: "Everyman, stand still."

Stalled by the traffic, waiting for the light
And giving a little at the knees, I stand
As still at others tied up in their shoes.
Looking ahead, my eyes switch out of sight,
Commemorating death by doing nothing
And needing a signal to get over it.

Behind my packages, I sweat it out,
Having already memorized the corner—
The fireplug, street-sign, waste-can, cracked cement
With which our city civilizes dirt—
And, feeling cornered, shuffle to keep warm,
Knowing it's useless now to plant my feet.

Ahead of me, all out from under arrest
And rushing suddenly over the jammed street,
The others hurry off to make up time;
But losing this moment, Death, I wait for you
To let me go. My disobedient body
Clings to my spine like a drunk to a lamppost.

Night Passage

The lights are going on over the water.
Over the ridge of the disappearing island
Headlights rise and fall like the ledge of the sun,
And starlight shiftier than eyes
Across the headland flashes the end of day.

Out of the houses and the fading woods,
On the water (scarlet
For rocks and the glimmering starboard landfall)
From the depths, the burning creatures come,
Their luminous slow heads touching the night.

Lights coming on in the dark look out of holes
At others burnt to sleep in the distance,
My mind, going out among them, going out.

By the Orchard

Rushing through leaves, they fall
Down, abruptly down
To the ground, bumping the branches,
The windfall apples falling
Yellow into the long grass and lying
Where they have fallen
In the tree's shadow, the shades
Of their soft bruises sinking, opening wide
Mouths to the mouths of creatures
Who like the sun are falling
To flicker, to worm's end under
Themselves, the hatch of moons.

Going to Pieces

Pull yourself together, pal.
—advice from a stranger

Those marionette-show skeletons can do it
Suddenly, after their skulls have been
Alone in the rafters, after their wishbones
Have fluttered in the wings, leaving the feet onstage
To hoof it solo: they pull themselves together,
Bring everything back and thread it on their spines.

But looking around and seeing other people
Coming apart at parties, breaking up
And catching their own laughter in both hands,
Or crossing the lawn and throwing up their spirits
Like voice-balloons in funnies, touching noses
In bedroom mirrors, one after another,
I figure something can be said for it:
Maybe some people break in better halves
Or some of the parts are greater than the whole.

Pal, take a look around: a heap of coats
Discarded in one spot like empty skins;
Under the tables enough shoes and gloves,
Enough loose hair, saliva, and fingernails
To conjure bodies off a hundred souls.
Now I'll tell *you* one: the palolo worms,
One night a year at the bottom of the sea,
Back halfway out of the burrows where they spend
Long lives; their tails turn luminous, twist free,
And all by themselves swim up to the surface,
Joining with millions of other detached tails;
The sea in a writhing mass lies white for miles
Under a gibbous moon; the bright halves die
And float away like scraps after a party,
But leave behind their larvae, set for life.

90

Meanwhile, the old ones, steady in their holes
Can go about their business, fanning food
Into their sleek, uninterrupted gullets.
Think of them there, pal, chewing the ocean,
Staying alive by going to pieces.

Stretching Canvases

By the last of the light, I pull
Over firm stretcher-bars
The ends of the last canvas
You wanted, miter the corners
Like sheets on a guest-bed,
And staple them on tight.
Stark white, three in a row
Are leaning on our house
To catch at the sunset.
From their surfaces, the stream
Of the undivided spectrum—
The whole palette of light—
Has put out both my eyes.
Good luck, my darling.
I can't see a thing.
My hammer flustered crows
All afternoon, kept jays
Out of the hazel trees.
I'm an aimless carpenter,
And now it's going to be winter
By the rule of this blue thumb.
We need storm-windows
In frames exactly like these.
Good luck to the canvas
Under the boxer's back
And the sail over the circus;
And good luck, facing you,
To the three against the wall
Which may be windows yet.
Keeping the storms in mind
And brushing the sky light
Like the stubble of the wind,
Look through, darling, look through.

The Welcome

For leagues the bunting rose on telephone wires,
And we made way like gates, giving away
Everything handy, gingering old horses
And pressing back as plastered as posters
Against the shop-fronts, spilling their bargains.
Balloons blew wholesale out of the mouths of tubas,
Billboards collapsed on multicolored hams,
And we waited. His lunch lay thawed in restaurants,
His cushions plumped, the girls asleep in cakes,
The corks already popped out of his magnums.
Our faces, all one way, went on and off
Like blinkers down the deserted lanes of the street.
Slowly the peach and lavender gulls stopped flying.

And he arrived on the wrong side of town
With no doors sighing open, no rushing lipstick,
And no quick squeezes for the quick or the dead.
Jaywalking over rails and safety-islands,
Through lawns and alleys, bumping barbecues
And shuffling straight through hedges and ash piles,
Trespassing yards with dogs dogging his heels,
Through summer mulch, the vee's of broken clotheslines
Following him like geese over our fences,
He slipped into the vacant heart of the city
And out the other side without a word.

Revival

for Richard Hugo

When Brother Jessen showed the tawny spot
On the carpet where a man threw up a demon,
He had another man by the ear
Beside the rose-covered plastic cross. He shouted
Into that ear a dozen times in a row,
"I curse you, Demon, in the name of Jesus!"
Some of his flock clapped hands. He knelt and sweated.
"They can try skating and wienie roasts," he said,
"But that don't keep the kids out of lovers' lane."
He pointed at me. "You don't believe in demons."

Next door, they were chasing some with double shots,
And the wind was up, and it was one of those nights
When it's hard to breathe
And you can't sit still or talk, when your eyes focus
On all disjointed scraps shoved into corners,
And something's going to happen. People feel fine,
Brother Jessen says, if they can lose their demons.
They wash in showers of everlasting dew
Which is the sweat of angels sick for men.

The demon has names, he told me, like Rebellion,
And it won't submit, it wants a cup of coffee,
Wants to go for a walk, and like as not
Turns up in Hell. Hugo, if you and I,
Having been cursed by some tough guy like Jesus,
Were to lose that wild, squat, bloody, grinning demon
Locked in the pit of our respective guts,
Whose fork has pitched us, flattened us to walls,
Left us in alleys where the moon smells dead,
Or jerked us out of the arms of our wives to write
Something like this, we'd sprawl flat on the floor,
A couple of tame spots at a revival.

Let's save a little sweat for the bad guys
Who can't keep out of lovers' lane for a minute,
Who, when they trip, will lie there in the rut
For old time's sake, rebellious as all Hell,
Croaking forever, loving the hard way.

Talking to the Forest

"When we can understand animals, we will know the change is halfway. When we can talk to the forest, we will know that the change has come."
—Andrew Joe, Skagit Tribe, Washington

We'll notice first they've quit turning their ears
To catch our voices drifting through cage-bars,
The whites of their eyes no longer shining from corners.
And all dumb animals suddenly struck dumb
Will turn away, embarrassed by a change
Among our hoots and catcalls, whistles and snorts
That crowd the air as tightly as ground-mist.

The cassowary pacing the hurricane fence,
The owl on the driftwood, the gorilla with folding arms,
The buffalo aimed all day in one direction,
The bear on his rock—will need no talking to,
Spending their time so deeply wrapped in time
(Where words lie down like the lion and the lamb)
Not even their own language could reach them.

And so, we'll have to get out of the zoo
To the forest, rain or shine, whichever comes
Dropping its downright shafts before our eyes,
And think of something to say, using new words
That won't turn back bewildered, lost or scattered
Or panicked, curling under the first bush
To wait for a loud voice to hunt them out,

Not words that fall from the skin looking like water
And running together, meaning anything,
Then disappearing into the forest floor
Through gray-green moss and ferns rotting in shade,
Not words like crown-fire overhead, but words
Like old trees felled by themselves in the wilderness,
Making no noise unless someone is listening.

Walking in the Snow

". . . if the author had said, 'Let us put on appropriate galoshes,'
there could, of course, have been no poem . . ."
—an analysis of Elinor Wylie's "Velvet Shoes,"
College English, *March 1948, p. 319.*

Let us put on appropriate galoshes, letting them flap open,
And walk in the snow.
The eyes have fallen out of the nearest snowman;
It slumps in its shadow,
And the slush at the curb is gray as the breasts of gulls.
As we slog together
Past arbors and stiff trees, all knocked out cold
At the broken end of winter,
No matter what may be falling out of the sky
Or blowing sideways
Against our hearts, we'll make up our own weather.
Love, stamping our galoshes,
Let's say something inappropriate, something flat
As a scholar's ear
And, since this can't be a poem, something loud
And pointless, leading nowhere
Like our footprints ducking and draking in the snow
One after the other.

An Afternoon on the Ground

The ducks and the green drakes
Covered flooded fields.
The herons struck themselves
Aslant in the flowing moss,
And pinetrees, burnt with crows,
Stood short of the mountains.
One hawk rose through the sun,
Casting no shadow down.

These thoughts were five miles long,
Stretched on a river road
Over a frail bridge
Past swampland and meadow
To the prison's honor farm
Where, ghost-pale to the waist,
Running in bare feet,
The trusties were playing ball.

How could I hold them all
Between the sides of my head?
The ducks were as good as gone,
The river would calm down,
The frogs and herons would fly
Together or separately
Like water through the air
Or air over the water,
And the crows all scatter
And the mountain behind them
Be a mountain in a poem
Off which nothing could fall,
And the hawk turn into feathers.

Along that stretch of river
For five miles, hanging on
To the truth of the matter
That led from birds to men,
I had trailed it after me.
But suddenly it tightened.
The end slipped out of my mind,
And the bare-backed prisoners
Were running around a field
On the first good day of spring,
Lifting their arms and shouting.

Sleeping by a River

My feet cut off from me, the ends of my legs
As heavy as the stones they're lying on,
One hand cupped empty over my forehead,
I wake by the riverside, catching myself
Napping, open-mouthed under a cloud.

A rock stuck in my back like a revolver
Holds me up a moment, lets me down
To this numb heap of matter
Whose pieces won't rouse out. I should have known
Better than this. There isn't one dumb creature

Back in the woods who'd fall asleep out here.
There's too much give and take out in the open.
Someone moved the sun when I wasn't looking
And did me to a turn as red as leaves.
Here come the flies across the hatch of evening.

And something drank my spirits while I slept,
Then corked me like a bottle without a message.
It coaxed the soul out of my fingertips,
Spun out its prints as vaguely as whirlpools,
Rippled across my forehead, and flew off.

I shift my upper eye to see the crows
Leaving an alder, full of their dark selves.
This is the way it goes.
The soul goes straight away as the crow flies
With enough noise to wake what's left behind
And leave it, one eye up, like a dying salmon.

After Falling

Sleep lightly, sleep eventfully
That from the jangling backs of your eyes may come the
    harness
Without horses, the trappings of darkness
And a country in pieces wedged across pale hills
And out of the mind—through fields ragged with light
Where the wrong birds out of season
Crouch in the grass, their wings trembling like eyelids.

Sleep watchfully, now, leaning across
The long strands holding the night like reins through
    clouds
And darkening with them, flourishing into water
Where the rough road divides repeatedly,
Dissolving slowly, streaming over the ground
But springing again, as the birds will,
To climb through wilder country before falling.

A Valedictory to Standard Oil of Indiana

In the darkness east of Chicago, the sky burns over the
    plumbers' nightmares
Red and blue, and my hometown lies there loaded with
    gasoline.
Registers ring like gas-pumps, pumps like pinballs, pinballs like
    broken alarm clocks,
And it's time for morning, but nothing's going to work.
From cat-cracker to candle-shop, from grease-works along the
    pipeline,
Over storage tanks like kings on a checkerboard ready to jump
    the county,
The word goes out: With refined regrets
We suggest you sleep all day in your houses shaped like lunch
    buckets
And don't show up at the automated gates.
Something else will tap the gauges without yawning
And check the valves at the feet of the cooling-towers without
    complaining.
Standard Oil is canning my high school classmates
And the ones who fell out of junior high or slipped in the grades.
What should they do, gassed up in their Tempests and Comets,
    raring to go
Somewhere with their wives scowling in front and kids stuffed
    in the back,
Past drive-ins jammed like car-lots, trying to find the beaches
But blocked by freights for hours, stopped dead in their tracks
Where the rails, as thick as thieves along the lakefront,
Lower their crossing gates to shut the frontier? What can they
    think about
As they stare at the sides of boxcars for a sign,
And Lake Michigan drains slowly into Lake Huron,
The mills level the Dunes, and the eels go sailing through the
    trout,

And mosquitoes inherit the evening, while toads no bigger than
     horseflies
Hop crazily after them over the lawns and sidewalks, and the
     rainbows fall
Flat in the oil they came from? There are two towns now,
One dark, one going to be dark, divided by cyclone fences;
One pampered and cared for like pillboxes and cathedrals,
The other vanishing overnight in the dumps and swamps like a
     struck sideshow.
As the Laureate of the Class of '44—which doesn't know it has
     one—
I offer this poem, not from hustings or barricades
Or the rickety stage where George Rogers Clark stood glued to
     the wall,
But from another way out, like Barnum's "This Way to the
     Egress,"
Which moved the suckers when they'd seen enough. Get out of
     town.

The Circuit

My circuit-riding great-grandfather
Rode off on horseback through the hickory woods
Each week to galvanize five Methodist churches,
And once, passing a Sabbath-breaking auction,
Shouted over his shoulder, "Fifteen cents!"
They caught him miles away
And saddled him with an old grandfather clock.

What got you up on your horse in the morning, sir?
Did you rehearse damnation
Till the trees fell crossways like a corduroy road?
Did anyone catch his death, as you caught yours,
Coming to hear you freezing in a shed?
Nobody mentions anything you did
Except the clock—no name-dropping of God,
No chiming adage. A joke thrown back of a horse
Has lasted longer than your rules and reasons.

I saw you stiff as a tintype in your bed
Next to a basin and a worn-out Bible,
Your beard aimed at the ceiling like a sermon.
Over the distance I can hear you shouting,
"Where in the name of God is the Name of God
In all these damned unsingable useless poems?"

Your family fought harder for the clock
Than they did for souls, and now they know its face
Better than yours, having replaced the works.
Beards are no longer hanging out of pulpits;
If God speaks from a bush, it's only by chance.
I shave my face and wait,
But bid for every clock I lay my eyes on
Just for the hell of it, your Hell and mine.
Like you, I'm doing time in the hard woods,
Tracking myself in circles, a lost preacher.

Speech from a Comedy

Scene: The wreckage of Heaven

I am God. But all my creatures are unkind to me.
They think of themselves. Why don't they think of me?
I'm holier than they.
      Chorus   God is lovely.
If I descended and rode through the streets,
Would they take off their hats?
No, they'd keep their hands in each other's pockets.
      Chorus   God is out of sorts.
Or if I showed up to give a formal address
Including an enormous amount of sound, godly advice,
They'd turn and wriggle away like a school of fish.
      Chorus   God is endless.
I burned myself in a bush once. Day and night,
I burned like a pillar of virtue in the desert.
I even let them watch me ride in my chariot.
      Chorus   God is great.
I gave them Aaron's rod when they were on the rocks.
I plagued their enemies with a thousand dirty tricks.
I let them burn rams in thickets instead of their precious
    Isaacs.
      Chorus   God is on their backs.
When things looked so black they couldn't tell his from
    hers,
I parted the waters,
Saving a few. But drowning a lot of others.
      Chorus   God is feeling worse.
Didn't I die for them?
Hang myself? And shed the Blood of the Lamb?
What more could I do? Try it yourself sometime.
      Chorus   God is sublime.
Now they forsake me. Leave me up in the air.
Sinning. Thinking of pleasure.
The more I leave them alone, the worse they are.
      Chorus   God is pure.

105

They lie all night in their houses stacked in rows,
Their knees pulled up, their heads stuffed into pillows,
Imagining new ways to break my laws.
        Chorus   God is jealous.
When I show them a bad example, plastered and confused,
Chances are he'll be headlined and idolized.
The only law of mine they like is getting circumcised.
        Chorus   God is not amused.
I didn't ask for anything impossible.
I said, "Love me—and not just once in a while."
But all men were created fickle.
        Chorus   God is immortal.
I'll settle with Everyman.
I had his dinner all laid out in my mansion,
But *he* had to try cooking his *own*.
        Chorus   God is burning.
Just because angels are blasé and neuter,
Did he think I'd be contented forever and ever
Playing with Ezekiel's wheel or climbing up and down
      Jacob's ladder?
        Chorus   God is boiling over.
I made him in my image, didn't I?
I gave him my tooth for a tooth, my eye for an eye.
How could I turn out such an unreasonable facsimile?
        Chorus   God is mighty sorry.
He'll be made to see the way things really are.
If he's so fond of slaughter,
I can get it for him wholesale just by losing my temper.
        Chorus   God's a man-of-war.
I might have shown him mercy,
But nobody asked me.
The best things in Heaven are costly.
        Chorus   God is free.

All right, he's dug his bed. Now let him lie in it
A thousand years at a stretch on a strict diet
While worms with their noses on fire pay an endless visit.
        Chorus   God is like that.
I watched over him like a shepherd over a sheep
While he went bleating and gambolling and flocking
      around and getting fleeced, forgetting whom to
      worship.
Well, every shepherd knows his way to the butchershop.
        Chorus   God is in bad shape.
Come, Death. He has made me mad.
I summon Death. For his ingratitude,
Everyman must choke on his daily bread.
        Chorus   God is sick and tired.

The Osprey's Nest

The osprey's nest has dropped of its own weight
After years, breaking everything under it, collapsing
Out of the sky like the wreckage of the moon,
Having killed its branch and rotted its lodgepole:
A flying cloud of fishbones tall as a man,
A shambles of dead storms ten feet across.

Uncertain what holds anything together,
Ospreys try everything—fishnets and broomsticks,
Welcome-mats and pieces of scarecrows,
Sheep bones, shells, the folded wings of mallards—
And heap up generations till they topple.

In the nest the young ones, calling fish to fly
Over the water toward them in old talons,
Thought only of hunger diving down their throats
To the heart, not letting go—(not letting go,
Ospreys have washed ashore, ruffled and calm
But drowned, their claws embedded in salmon).
They saw the world was bones and curtain-rods,
Hay-wire and cornstalks—rubble put to bed
And glued into meaning by large appetites.
Living on top of everything that mattered,
The fledglings held it in the air with their eyes,
With awkward claws groping the ghosts of fish.

Last night they slapped themselves into the wind
And cried across the rain, flopping for comfort
Against the nearest branches, baffled by leaves
And the blank darkness falling below their breasts.
Where have they gone? The nest, now heaped on the
    bank,
Has come to earth smelling as high as heaven.

Making Up for a Soul

It's been like fixing a clock, jamming the wheels,
The pinions, and bent springs into a box
And shaking it. Or like patching a vase,
Gluing the mismatched edges of events
Together despite the quirks in the design.
Or trying to make one out of scraps of paper,
The yellowing, dog-eared pages going slapdash
Over each other, flat as a collage.
I can't keep time with it. It won't hold water.
Ripping and rearranging make no pattern.

Imagine me with a soul: I'm sitting here
In the room with you, smiling from corner to corner,
My chest going up and down with inspiration.
I sit serene, insufferably at my ease,
Not scratching or drumming but merely suffering
Your questions, like the man from the back of the book
With all the answers. You couldn't stand me, could you?

My love, if you have a soul, don't tell me yet.
Why can't we simply stay uneasy together?
There are snap-on souls like luminous neckties
That light up in the dark, spelling our names.
Let's put them on for solemn visitors,
Switch off the lights, then grope from room to room,
Making our hollow, diabolical noises
Like Dracula and his spouse, avoiding mirrors,
Clutching each other fiendishly for life
To stop the gaps in ourselves, like better halves.

Observations from the Outer Edge

I pass the abrupt end of the woods, and stop.
I'm standing on a cliff as sheer as a step
Where the ground, like the ground floor of a nightmare,
Has slipped a notch six hundred rocky feet
And left itself in the lurch. My shoes go dead.
Not looking yet, I let my heart sneak back,

But feel like the fall-guy ending a Western,
The heavy, bound to topple from the edge
And disappear with terrible gravity.
I put my hand out in the separate air
With nothing under it, but it feels nothing.
This is no place for putting my foot down,

So I shout my name, but can't scare up an echo.
No one inside this canyon wants to be me.
I manage to look down. Not much to envy:
The silent, immobile rapids, the toy pines,
A fisherman stuck in the shallows like an agate—
A world so far away, it could quit moving

And I wouldn't know the difference. I've seen it before
At the ends of hallways, the far sides of windows,
Shrinking from sight. Down is no worse than across.
Whether it's sky, horizon, or ground zero,
A piece of space will take whatever comes
From any direction—climbing, walking, or falling.

I remember a newsreel—a man holding a baby
Over the Grand Canyon on a stick:
The kid hung on and grinned for the camera.
I grab the nearest branch just to make sure
It isn't death down there, looking like hell.
Even a mountain goat will go to pieces

Standing on glass suspended in the air,
But man created with a jerkier balance
Can learn to fix his eyes on a safe place.
Trembling somewhere,
The acrophobiac Primum Mobile
Clings to his starry axle, staring sideways.

Leaving Something Behind

A fox at your neck and snakeskin on your feet,
You have gone to the city behind an ivory brooch,
Wearing your charms for and against desire, bearing your
    beauty
Past all the gaping doorways, amazing women on edge
And leading men's eyes astray while skirting mayhem,
And I, for a day, must wish you safe in your skin.

The diggers named her the Minnesota Girl. She was fifteen,
Eight thousand years ago, when she drowned in a glacial
    lake,
Curling to sleep like her sea-snail amulet, holding a
    turtleshell,
A wolf's tooth, the tine of an antler, carrying somehow
A dozen bones from the feet of water birds. She believed
    in her charms,
But something found her and kept her. She became what
    she wore.

She loved her bones and her own husk of creatures
But left them piecemeal on the branching shore.
Without you, fox paws, elephant haunches, all rattling tails,
Snails' feet, turtles' remote hearts, muzzles of wolves,
Stags' ears, and the tongues of water birds are only
    themselves.
Come safely back. There was nothing in her arms.

Working Against Time

By the newly bulldozed logging road, for a hundred yards,
I saw the sprawling five-foot hemlocks, their branches
    crammed
Into each other's light, upended or wrenched aslant
Or broken across waists the size of broomsticks
Or bent, crushed slewfoot on themselves in the duff like
    briars,
Their roots coming at random out of the dirt, and dying.

I had no burlap in the trunk, not even a spade,
And the shirt off my back wasn't enough to go around.
I'm no tree surgeon, it wasn't Arbor Day, but I climbed
Over the free-for-all, untangling winners and losers
And squeezing as many as I could into my car.
When I started, nothing was singing in the woods except me.

I hardly had room to steer—roots dangled over my shoulder
And scraped the side of my throat as if looking for water.
Branches against the fog on the windshield dabbled designs
Like kids or hung out the vent. The sun was falling down.
It's against the law to dig up trees. Working against
Time and across laws, I drove my ambulance

Forty miles in the dark to the house and began digging
Knee-deep graves for most of them, while the splayed
    headlights
Along the highway picked me out of the night:
A fool with a shovel searching for worms or treasure,
Both buried behind the sweat on his forehead. Two green
    survivors
Are tangled under the biting rain as I say this.

A Room with a View

1

At last, outside my window an expanse
For the mind's elbows, stretching north and south:
Houseboats and towers, drydocks and seaplanes,
Streets vaulting over hillsides
And the top of the sky pushed backward through the
    clouds,
Then over high bridges into the distance
Where the sun is breaking, falling beyond the mountains.

In the darkness, blazing like campfires locked in glass,
The lights from other houses
Survive the invisible weather of the night.
I watch through the dawn
Cars butting each other down long chutes to the city
And the black-decked seiner circling the inlet,
Dragging its purse behind, then slewing away
With the morning offering, leaving the water empty.

2

Looking up from a book or half a sentence
For some way out, I've seen from other rooms
Weeds sloping up to brambles, telephone wires,
Or strips of grass like runners between neighbors,
Or only the sweating windows
Themselves, as blank as paper, or streaky shades
Like moths too big and battered to get out.

Now the reach and stretch of this astounding air
Unfocuses my eyes. Whatever is coming
Must come from as far away as the horizon.
To see what I could only imagine once
When, shut in a box, I heard hard winter knocking,
Makes me afraid. Having set myself to think,

Having arranged to watch the weather coming,
I'm afraid it won't be real:
The wind in a single lane, the clouds in rows,
The lightning mastered in an orderly sheaf,
The snow and sleet in clusters,
The uniform thunder rolling itself flat.

A man in a room with a view draws back—
As though on a cliff—from the edge of the operatic,
Tempted to own it, to get above himself.
Poets and *helden* tenors, straining for height,
Mistake the roaring in their ears for the ocean.

3
In a small glass box I've made a terrarium:
Eight kinds of moss from the banks of mountain streams
Whose interlacing fern-like leaves
And outflung sporophytes like spears in a mob-scene
Make perfect sense from only a foot away,
As unpredictably various as a shrine
In a Zen garden, or a piece of forest floor
Where every inch of the dead is crammed with blossoms.

If I grew tired as a god and forgot its water
Or dumped it out the window
Or set out scientifically to destroy it
By fire or drowning or some kind of mayhem,
The least fragment, a half-burnt speck or spore
Or the most unlikely single rootless cell,
Where the green goes dark as night, could breed again
An entire garden. Here, pressed against the glass
On four high sides like the corners of the world,
It breathes my breath. Its weather is my face.

Come Before His Countenance
with a Joyful Leaping

Swivelling flat-soled on the dirt but ready to bound in arches
   at the nick of time, spurring yourselves, come all as
   you are with footbones rattling like claques, with
   storking knees careering into the crooked distance,
   horning in and out of sight,
Come coasting in circles, rearing, running aground, and
   flickering up the air, peeling and flaking away like
   handbills over the sloping daylight,
Come lambing and fishing, outflanking the body's heights at a
   single stroke, out of breath, out at the elbows,
   spreading blank palms and flinching up hillsides
   hoisted out of mind,
Come at a loss out of manholes and sandtraps, jerking free at
   the heart, assaulted and blinking on dislocated ankles,
   swollen with song from the twisted wreckage, dying
   and rigorous after the second wind,
For He is falling apart in His unstrung parbuckles, His beard
   blown loose by harmonious unction, His countenance
   breaking, His fragments flopping up and around
   without us to the stretches of morning.

Song to Accompany
the Bearer of Bad News

Kings kill their messengers
Sometimes, slicing wildly
Through pages delivering their grief
And you may do the same
With this page under this poem
Tear it lengthwise first
With feeling, cutting off
Each phrase into meaningless halves
Then crossways, severing
The mild beginning from the bad ending
By now you know the worst
Having imagined the remainder
Down to the painful inch
Where something like your name
Closes this message
You needn't finish now
You may stop here
And puzzle it out later.

Kings kill
Sometimes, slicing
Through pages
And you may
With this page
Tear it
With feeling
Each phrase
Then crossways
The mild beginning
By now you know
Having imagined
Down to

117

Where something
Closes
You needn't finish
You may stop
And puzzle it out.

Their messengers
Wildly
Delivering their grief
Do the same
Under this poem
Lengthwise first
Cutting off
Into meaningless halves
Severing
The bad ending
The worst
The remainder
The painful inch
Like your name
This message
Now
Here
Later

You may   tear it   into meaningless halves
Lengthwise first   then crossways
Severing   something like   the painful inch
Later   under this poem   messengers
Delivering their grief   puzzle it out
Having imagined   the worst
Kings kill   wildly   through pages

Cutting off   the bad ending
Do the same   with this page
By now you know   the mild beginning
Down to where   your name   closes
With feeling   now   you may stop.

New Poems

At St. Vincent DePaul's

"Free shoes, help yourself"

Buckling their thin soles,
These squads of shoes
In lines under the rain
Are shining this morning,
Rocking on round heels
Or turning up at the toes
As if to jump for joy
Or jump out of the way:
Oxfords and safety shoes
And boots whose arches fell
Flatter than handprints
Are warping back to life,
The cracked and wrinkled hides
As supple as fishskins
Now in the falling water
Under their own steam
Like the rising ghosts of socks,
The sneakers stuck together,
Slippers whose pompons
Bloom like anemones,
Golf shoes for trespassing,
The tongueless, the mismatched
For an hour helping themselves,
Free as long as they last.

Magic Night at the Reformatory

We're here because we're here, and the gray-haired
  salesman begins
Our act with coins, plucking them out of the air
With his white fingers;
And in this room, in this building, in a reformatory,
All the young men sit still in their folding chairs
To see him making
Something from nothing. When he coughs, the coins spill
  out of his nose
Into a nickel-plated bucket. He grins.
What am I doing
Grinning here with the others, shaking, waiting my turn,
Sweating it out at the edge of the platform?
The trick is showing
Your teeth at the right time. What Every Boy Should Know.
The applause goes on, then off; they pass it out,
Then jerk it back,
Looking around to see what the others are putting or taking.
The money shines in their eyes; they purse their mouths.
Now the fat banker
Is tearing a newspaper down and crossways, dividing
The Who from How and cutting the bad news
In half again and again
To a wad the size of a wallet and then unfolding it whole.
"For God's sake, don't teach them anything they can use,"
The warden said,
"And no female assistants." Deadpanned, they slump in
  their seats,
Not being fooled, not being taken in.
The doctor cuts a rope,
Knots it, restores it, and bumbles offstage, dropping his
  scissors.
The architect conjures doves from a warming pan,
And one flaps up,
Goes skittering around the windowless room, flies back

To become a squab which he gnaws for an exit.
And then I'm on
With only a deck of cards, watching my hands grow thick
Through waterfall and accordion shuffles, fans,
Sloppy arm-turnovers,
And color changes I learned when I was too young and too lucky
To get arrested except on Hallowe'en.
I remember friends
Who taught me to steal books, then how to write them.
What kind of sleight-of-hand will work tomorrow?
What kind of example
Were we supposed to be? The white, Indian, and Negro
Faces are watching to see what we can do,
If anything—
Production, destruction, restoration, illusion, manipulation,
With no intermission, with nothing usable
In a house of correction,
And I finish by throwing cards with a flick of the wrist,
    skimming
One after the other over their heads
And into the dark
At the back of the room where they smack into the wall,
    then drop
To the floor like sparrows conking themselves on glass.
The random applause
Says nothing to anyone. The lights go on. One Indian
Is trying to throw a card with a flick of the wrist.
It sticks in his fingers.
And we, the nervous Society of American Magicians,
Cluster to talk about ourselves. The guards
Reform the audience
And file it loud and long through a corridor, to vanish.
Under the floodlit night, we stroll to the gate
Which opens as if by magic.

Bums at Breakfast

Daily, the bums sat down to eat in our kitchen.
They seemed to be whatever the day was like:
If it was hot or cold, they were hot or cold;
If it was wet, they came in dripping wet.
One left his snowy shoes on the back porch
But his socks stuck to the clean linoleum,
And one, when my mother led him to the sink,
Wrung out his hat instead of washing his hands.

My father said they'd made a mark on the house,
A hobo's sign on the sidewalk, pointing the way.
I hunted everywhere, but never found it.
It must have said, "It's only good in the morning—
When the husband's out." My father knew by heart
Lectures on Thrift and Doggedness,
But he was always either working or sleeping.
My mother didn't know any advice.

They ate their food politely, with old hands,
Not looking around, and spoke in short, plain answers.
Sometimes they said what they'd been doing lately
Or told us what was wrong; but listening hard,
I broke their language into secret codes:
Their *east* meant *west*, their *job* meant *walking and
        walking,*
Their *money* meant *danger, home* meant *running and
        hiding,*
Their *father* and *mother* were different kinds of *weather.*

Dumbly, I watched them leave by the back door,
Their pockets empty as a ten-year-old's;
Yet they looked twice as rich, being full of breakfast.
I carried mine like a lump all the way to school.

When I was growing hungry, where would they be?
None ever came twice. Never to lunch or dinner.
They were always starting fresh in the fresh morning.
I dreamed of days that stopped at the beginning.

Blues to Be Sung in a Dark Voice

It's time to shine the bottom of my shoes.
Move over, cousin. Here comes my bad news.
Goodbye, good boy. Hello, hello, blues.
        spoken   Milkman won't milk me, tailor won't
                 suit me now.
So goodbye, good boy.

Florist won't let me smell his kind of bunch.
Grocer won't deliver me, that's a cinch.
Banker won't check me out to drink some lunch.
        spoken   Jeweler just watches, he don't ring
                 me up.
So goodbye, good boy.

Dealer won't cut me in on his old game.
Sheriff don't teach me how to spell my name.
Driver won't bus me, I'll get there just the same.
        spoken   Garbageman don't give me no
                 pick-me-ups.
So goodbye, good boy.

Shoe-man won't put bottoms on my tops.
Druggist drug me down to see the cops.
Plumber won't bail me out, I'm here for keeps.
        spoken   Railroads won't forgive my
                 trespasses.
So goodbye, good boy.

Baker ain't going to roll me any more.
Barber ain't going to clip me like before.
Mama can't get my knees down on the floor.
        spoken   Doctor won't take my pulse 'cause he
                 can't keep it.
So goodbye, good boy.

Loan-man likes that X on the dotted line.
Preacher, he keeps crossing me all the time:
Someone sets fire to it, it burns just fine.
        spoken   Landlord ain't going to land on me
                 again, Lord.
So goodbye, good boy.

The March of Coxey's Army

Massillon, Ohio, to Washington
—March 24 to May 1, 1894

They started on Easter Sunday like resurrected nobodies.
It was snowing into the chuck wagons, into the split drum
    and the tubas.
Before they blew out of town, someone counted a hundred noses.
    The taverns were shut as tight as a Presbyterian,
    And respectable doors were latched and keyholes corked all
        over Massillon
    Which on Sunday wouldn't even spell sarsaparilla in front of
        a deacon.
They came from all over the dusty map, gimp-legged and
        tatterdemalion,
Out of work, out at heels, out of boxcars, weak from eating
        slumgullion,
Ready to walk from Hell to breakfast and from breakfast to
        Washington.
    Two million men that winter were standing in bread-lines
    While gentlemen sucked their teeth and twiddled their gold
        watch-chains,
    Havanas between muttonchops, vests covered with dollar
        signs.
General Jacob Coxey from his carriage saw a country managed by
        halfwits,
By boodlers and credit-jugglers and quick-silver plutocrats,
Coupon-clippers and shufflers of imaginary banknotes.
    He saw the banks were scratching out confidence money
    Which stood for dollars whenever they didn't have any
    Or which stood for nothing whenever the banks felt slippery.
His daughter Mamie was bawling in the attic because she had to
        stay home.
Jesse, his son, was galloping around in an old Civil War uniform.
His grim wife rode in a carriage, rocking the baby Legal Tender in
        one arm.

The buglers and astrologers, Chicago cowboys and Toledo
      Indians started off
Behind Greasy Browne (his sombrero, his beard, and his
      manifesto the color of snuff)
With "The Dog Who Never Deserts the Flag" chained to the
      flagstaff.
From first to last, each footstep, each turn of a wagonwheel
Was a lurch from brick to rock, from rut to mudhole.
The road went east, and the wind came west to freeze its whistle.
      At first the band played "After the Ball Is Over" smack on the
          beat,
      But you can't march to a waltz unless you've got three feet,
      So they boomed and blared "Where Is My Wand'ring Boy
          Tonight?"
They had no bombs, but most had beards and nearly a dozen had
      overcoats,
And they all had lank faces and underfed gullets.
The general said, "Congress tears up pieces of paper, not Petitions
      in Boots!"
      The first mile, the first noon, the first night, men sat down to
          mull it over
      And didn't catch up. But others came, and like a sluggish river
      The march went on, though it was always different water.
The snow got tired and quit. And evening after evening
Sheriffs and paunchy deputies came out to keep them going
Sore foot after foot to the nearest county line.
      They looked at the freezing farms and the melting houses,
      They looked at people by the road, and people looked back
          with uncertain faces.
      At night they looked for stars, but saw the ends of their noses.
And they were surprised each morning under the baggy tents
To find each other there, eating hardtack, hitching up their pants,

And suddenly they had no room for lap-dogs, taffy-pullers, and
      house-plants.
   The wealthy General wore his homburg, foulard tie, and
      morning trousers
   And didn't try rednecking his way around the workers.
   And he slept in hotels on the march and not on cinders.
But he had them chanting, "Work for the Unemployed and Food
      for the Indigent!"
And "If Banks Let Us Down, We're Up to the Government!"
And "We're Sunk If We Keep Inflating and Money Doesn't!"
   And "The Unemployed Can Make Gardens Out of
      Battlegrounds!"
   And "The Unemployed Can Build Highways If Nobody Ties
      Their Hands!"
   And "He Rose On Easter, But Death To Interest On Bonds!"
Were they out of their minds? They were out of the State of Ohio,
      heading down
Where smoke was exploding like shellfire on the horizon,
To a blistered valley where the air stood thick as policemen.
   Men burnt the color of pig-iron came out of the half-shut
      mills to wave.
   They stood in somebody else's Homestead, keeping a few
      jobs, staying alive.
   And the companies minded everyone's manners with the
      business-end of a sheriff.
The marchers kept their heads for miles between silent rows
Of loaded militia who were aching to keep the peace,
While newspapers shouted, A PLAGUE OF LOCUSTS and
      A MARCH OF DISEASE!
   And somehow they didn't catch typhus on the banks of the
      Ohio.
   Sometimes the river would back up, sometimes it would flow.
   It was close enough to smell, but too thick to jump into.

And Greasy Browne shouted, "A thousand bums going in one
        direction instead of nowhere!
A thousand bums with their stomachs growling for supper!
If we had a thousand bums, we'd raise a stink like a pillar of fire!"
      And "If every gun in the country backfired, you wouldn't
          scratch a bum."
      And "Give every bum a bath and a haircut, and kill your
          society column."
      And "The General's the Cerebrum of Christ and I'm the
          Cerebellum!"
He could give an evangelical chalk-talk that doubled up reporters.
He painted the haloed head of Christ on one of his posters
And gave it calculating, squinty eyes and his own whiskers.
      But the General said, "When your belly's empty, you can't
          stand belly-laughs.
      Laughs won't pull Congressmen's pig-knuckles out of their
          troughs.
      And you can't blow down their marble pig-pens with huffs
          and puffs."
In photographs, they slump in their bowlers and striped shirts,
Shaving each other or strewn under canvas like a wrecked circus.
But as the weeks crawled by, they crawled slowly southeast.
      There lay the Allegheny Mountains crumpled like soggy
          cardboard.
      Men came and men quit, but there were two hundred
      Scraping themselves uphill, even when the wind turned solid.
They felt forgotten, but got over it and into Maryland
Through snowdrifts and insurrections, leaving behind
Reporters, unbroken windows, live chickens, old clothes, and
          friends.
      They lived off the uneasy land, breaking some laws
      Like trespassing, parading without permits, and thinking on
          Sundays.

When they came to the last river, they were headline news.
They spent two days and two nights in barges on the Potomac
Till their faces looked greener than Martha Washington's on a
greenback.
Each could have thrown a silver dollar across, if he'd had it in his
stomach.
But they grew fresher and brighter, tramping toward
Washington.
When they camped on the last of April, five hundred strong,
They dusted their hair, stiffened their backs, and cranked up
the dawn.
The ranks were loaded with Secret Servicemen,
Spies, and pipe-sucking Pinkerton agents, according to Greasy
Browne.
The General said, "They've come to school, they'll stay for
graduation."
President Grover Cleveland stood up and started smoking.
Senator William Jennings Bryan sat down and stopped talking.
But Brigadier General Ordway ordered everyone to start
countermarching.
"No parades and no banners," said the D. of C. Chief of Police,
But here came runaway Mamie Coxey dressed as the Goddess of
Peace
With 30,000 people cheering and her hair tickling her knees.
She was shocking her mother at the bottom of her bent,
And the band was booming "Marching Through Georgia"
with an Ohio accent,
Yet the marchers were as good as gold when they passed the
Mint.
They wanted to go to the Capitol steps and hear the General
speak,
But suddenly there was a straight wall of policemen on horseback,
One for each marcher and some left over, each twirling a
nightstick.

Adjusting his pince-nez and saying, "Excuse me, please,"
The General cut to his left and, zigzagging like Congress,
Crossed to the Capitol steps on a carpet of grass.
His speech was still in his hand when he was arrested.
"Here's where Kings and Princes have wiped their feet," it said.
"Here's where the fat-necked lobbyists have been red-carpeted."
And hundreds of billyclubs went up and came down
On scalps and derbies, on temples and collarbones.
When the dust blew off, "The Dog Who Never Deserts the
    Flag" had broken its chain.
And the march was going in all directions, into poolrooms and
    hospitals,
Into taverns and city parks, into boxcars and jails,
Into the air, into the backs of minds. It was scattered like
    handbills.
People strolled home or went groggy to dinner.
Some looked at the blood. Some looked at themselves. Some
    looked at 1894.
The General got twenty days for walking on the grass, and the
    show was over.

Searching in the Britannia Tavern

to Earl Lund, Clallam Tribe, Washington

To get to the land of the dead, you must go through
The place where everything is flying, past falling water
To the curb, across the sidewalk, stumbling, to the hunting
    ground;
Sleeping by day and moving only by night, you will come
To the place where you must sink, then rise, then enter
The abrupt silence where they have hidden your soul.

Having no one to be, the dead steal souls. They lie
In wait in the middle of the floor, or spraddle for balance,
Their eyes burnt out. Those climbing toward the door
Have never entered. Those descending never arrive. They stand
Facing in different directions, blinking at walls, remembering
Nothing about your life. Remember, you told me,

Only your spirit can grapple with the dead.
It must be danced or it never appears. You must watch for it
At night, or walk all day in your sleep, or stay under water
To make it come to you. When it enters, nothing stands still.
The wall is the floor, the floor and ceiling are walls,
Its voice is breaking in your ears, its broken speech

Is saying what you must know, the dead are falling
Against each other, rattling their helpless fingers, remember,
The First People changed into bears, into rocks and fish,
Into trees, beavers, and birds, when they learned that men
    were coming,
And there, stalking toward you, the dark one is
    Tah-mah-no-us,
One Who Has Never Changed, his terrible mouth is smiling,
    he bears
Your soul slowly toward you in cupped hands.

Getting Out of Jail on Monday

I'm going into the building, he's coming out.
It's City Property where official cement
Pours sideways, up, and down out of the windows.
I'm paying fines for driving and walking crooked
And he's getting out of jail on a fine morning,
Singing and waving, just walking away.

As if he'd sung my name, I turn and follow
This husky, bowlegged, upright, sockless Indian
Who's singing, going downhill as straight as an arrow.
He's chanting deep in his throat, his mouth hangs open
Like that tavern doorway. Stomping, he sings against it
As harsh and sharp as the wind through underbrush.

The sun is sunnyside up, swatches of sky
Are glancing down from the windows around us,
The gutter's a foot away, the secretaries
Are sharpening the corners of their eyes,
The boards are busy upstairs, good signatures
Are flourishing at the business-ends of letters,

And the Indian goes inside like a parade.
Me too. I buy him a beer. He sings around it,
Staring at me with flat obsidian eyes,
Then drinks it aloud. The sun is over easy.
I buy another, we down it against the clock
Which is prying the hour apart with its bare hands.

All over town the time-vaults are yawning open.
They disengage their polished, case-hardened teeth
From the dark strikes that bolted them all home.
The money is rolling out into the morning
After a breathless weekend in the tank.
The jukebox crackles and burns in the corner.

137

I give him my necktie. He threads it like a belt
And hikes his pants, cinching himself tight.
We try to imagine not being arrested
Till the end of the week. I tell him about work,
And we drink to cinches tighter than our luck.
Outside, the sun is a raw egg in a beer,

And the cars and cabs are jerking around noon.
From this enormous distance, you have to shout
To make yourself heard. You have to pay a fine
For singing or shouting crooked at a machine.
With five days off and two in a safe place,
We're like an investment. The Indian backs me up.

He backs me up against the front of the tavern
And does a dance with his hair in his face. I explain
To people scuttling around him what he means.
He means he's working at dancing through the week
And staring at the burnt insides of eyelids
With a stomach full of the City and no socks.

Machines are cranking mimeographed Tuesdays,
Tuesdays are sticking to Wednesdays, they're running
        off Thursdays
In case of increased demand, but Fridays go blank,
And trying to see Friday west of Monday
Takes an Indian's eyes. It's over the brow of the hill
Like the U.S. Cavalry with its spit and tarnish,

And suddenly dancing, I'm Big Medicine.
I prophesy: Nothing is going to work
Till it sings for itself. Hundreds of want-ads
Are flying from Pioneer Square to Puget Sound
Like seagulls. The beak of Thunderbird is breaking
On Killer Whale, we all light up in the rain,

And it puts us out. The sun is scrambling off.
The Indian rattles away through a strange language.
Slowly my arches sink back to the pavement.
My hair sits down, my chin warps shut like a drawer.
I put the touch on myself and start uphill,
A solid citizen, going to pay on time.

The Burglar

Being a burglar, you slip out of doors in the morning
And look at the street by looking at the sky,
Not being taken in by anything blue.
You must look to the left or right to see across.
If nothing strikes your eye, if no one comes running,
You've stolen another day.

You must spend it on your toes
At the edges of buildings, doorways, and windows
Wherever no one is watching close enough.
Keep your fingers light as smoke.
You may have permission to kiss with one eye open.
Try every door while leaning away from it.

But sundown is serious; it's time to go home
To the house that will draw you under its empty wing.
Climbing like ivy up the drains, go through
The furthest window into a dark room.
Wait there to hear how everything has gone.
Then, masking every motion,

Glide to the stairwell.
They will be eating dinner: the man and the woman
At opposite ends of a white and silver table;
Between them, food and candles and children.
Their knives and forks go in and out of their mouths;
Whatever they do will aim them toward each other.

Now, follow your fingerprints around all corners
From nightlatch to velvet lid, from hasp to stone.
Everything locked, of course, has been locked for you:
You must break in softly, take whatever you find
Whether you understand what it is or not.
Breathe in, reach out,

Stealing one thing at a time.
If you grow hungry, thinking of their desserts,
It's time to vanish over the windowsill.
You must go without their dinner into the night,
Not saying goodbye, not waiting to scrawl a note
To say you're running away, but running away.

The Shoplifter

She stands alone in the aisle, head tilted
As if listening to women, the women
Glittering or moping past her
Among the gloves and purses, glancing like light
On necklaces, half clear, half dreaming.

Everyone is here; no one is watching—
Children and loud mothers, the girls in black,
The manager erect among questions.
Languidly her hand moves
Over the counter. Now it is touching

Something, lifting it, taking, and hiding.
Wherever it goes now, she darkens it.
She walks along the rows to the blurred
Revolving door, turning herself out.
The sun is melting like wax over the sidewalk.

Now a man stops her, holds her tightly.
A flush comes up across her face like a veil.
He brings her back alive; his hand
Is firm on her elbow, leading her up the aisle.
No one is here, but everyone is watching.

She is floating sideways, being drawn
Into the ceremonious distance, away from us.
Rising along the stairway, looking back,
She smiles serenely against the light.
The shop is lifting, lifting itself with her.

The Hold-Up

First comes a fence, then the mouth of an alley,
Then a shadow on the other side of shadows
Becomes a pole, a doorway, a garbage can
Becoming a bush with a voice becoming an arm
Holding a gun at my back. This is a hold-up.
We wait a moment. We listen
For whatever it might be I'm going to say.
The wind crawls out from under the parked cars.

My arms go up in the air. My hands turn white.
Apparently I won't be saying anything.
He empties the deep pocket over my heart,
Then pats my hips as if guessing my weight.
Half-turning, I see the stocking down his face
Erasing lips and eyes, smoothing his nose.
We pass the time of night together.
He does the breathing for both of us.

The muzzle touches my back
Gently, like the muzzle of a dog. What's holding me up?
Take off your shoes. I stand in stocking feet
On the cinders. He begins to fade.
I had been walking from streetlight to streetlight,
My shadow straight as a footbridge under me,
Forgetting the mouths of alleys by moonlight.
My shoes and my money are running away in the dark.

The Visiting Hour

Strip off your clothes and give them to a man
In a uniform, hurry to take a shower,
Put on a starchy, stark-white coverall
That can stand up by itself, then keeping in line,
March to the visitor's room.

It has lamps, rugs, curtains, movable furniture,
And a woman among some women, looking at you
And wearing a dress and holding out her arms
(Which may be entered against her)
And shutting and opening her mouth for an hour.

Standing behind his bullet-proof glass, the guard
Has been instructed to stare, but stares at the wall,
The ceiling, or between your bodies
As if recalling games on television.
What you can do is act like him for her:

Your eyes must look at something common between you—
A crack, a flower on a cushion.
Your hands may touch each other item by item
In order, checking down the list of reminders.
You may reach for almost anything but conclusions.

When a bell rings, there is nothing left to answer,
No one is calling or waiting, nothing is ready—
The time has simply gone, and the time has come
To say goodbye like scouts of opposing factions
From opposite closing doors.

From the corridor, you'll enter an empty room
To be stripped and searched for imaginary objects:
Stooping, squatting, and squinting, the guards go through
Your closets and blind alleys
To catch you keeping what you can never get.

The long way back will take you past a gate
Where you can see a man outside in a tower.
His searchlight, his eyes, his rifle
All turn toward you if you stop to wave.
He must know you to let you out. He doesn't know you.

And in Cell Block D, nobody wants to shoot you.
Those tiers with railings
Rise forty feet like the face of a motel
With ice on every floor. Like venetian blinds,
The catwalks show you mounting, kneeling, or lying.

The guards in the gallery simply look and listen
Over their sights if you thumb your nose or scream
Or try to throw something far enough to reach them.
They'll put your name on a list; then visitors
Will have to imagine you for years and years.

The Escape Artist

for Will Desmond

In the middle of the crowd, they're strapping him into it,
Straining and buckling as if over a madman.
Through the tapering, cuffless sleeves of the strait-jacket
He hugs himself to keep his body waiting.
The crane hums loudly between buildings. It hoists
The heavy hook between the straps at his ankles.
He smiles Goodbye, Goodbye, going upside down,
Red in the face, his hair standing on end.
The crowd below makes room for a mistake.

Hooked in the clear sky, he dangles
Like something restless dreaming about flying.
Inside the canvas, suddenly his forearms
Wrestling his sidling shoulders, his raw neck heaving
And doubling, everything writhing—his head comes
    breaching out
From the crooks of his elbows,
The buckles parting; his chest and arms break free
And he hangs flapping, a wet, half-folded moth.

From the street, nervous advice. Someone baits him.
Flashguns. Mouths gape as if being fed.
He peels himself, dropping the empty jacket.
The sweat rolls up his face and into his eyes
Like tears coming backward; his smile is wrong side up.
Slowly the cable lowers him on the hook,
Putting him back where he was, among us.

Tumbleweed

Here comes another, bumping over the sage
Among the greasewood, wobbling diagonally
Downhill, then skimming a moment on its edge,
Tilting lopsided, bouncing end over end
And springing from the puffs of its own dust
To catch at the barbed wire
And hang there, shaking, like a riddled prisoner.

Half the sharp seeds have fallen from this tumbler,
Knocked out for good by head-stands and pratfalls
Between here and wherever it grew up.
I carry it in the wind across the road
To the other fence. It jerks in my hands,
Butts backwards, corkscrews, lunges and swivels,
Then yaws away as soon as it's let go,
Hopping the scrub uphill like a kicked maverick.
The air goes hard and straight through the wires and
        weeds.
Here comes another, flopping among the sage.

The Soles

The soles are lying in shallows off Dungeness Spit.
They rest on vacant sides and stare at the sun.
Their skin like sand is glowing against the sand.

The tide has come and gone. It comes again.
The soles are lying still as their own breath.
The ocean passes through the straits of their gills.

One eye has moved an inch in a million years
To join the other on the burning side,
Drawn up like a moon from underlying night.

They dart and bury themselves as we drift over.
They cloud the sand across their speckled halves.
Their fixed, their wandering eyes stare up again.

Recollection

Dear, I have been days
Drudging at words. They lie
Wherever I put them down
As separate as stones.
There on the page, they are
Exactly what they are.

Only an hour ago
I was driving from nowhere
To nowhere in my car
When I remembered you—
As simply, as obviously
As men remember food
And turn from breaking stones
On stones, to break their bread.

This is the whole truth.
I stopped, and I sat down
On cinders, held my head
Together, took a drink
Of the unmanageable air
Where we first caught our breath,
And made this out of love.

Getting Above Ourselves
on Sunday

Here on this cliff, as high
As the heart of the weather,
We wait for it to break
Or stack its makeshift clouds
Into a storm. The rain
Is falling three ways at once;
And mottled, valley by valley
On clearing and outcrop,
The ramshackling light
Goes toppling through itself.
Wherever we can look,
Haphazard pieces of storm
Are smacking Haystack Mountain.
Dismantled thunderheads
Are tumbling, falling apart,
And breaking like seawrack
As close as our four feet.
Dust devils with no dust
Go needling through hemlocks,
Through a day made by a child
From whatever falls by chance
Into its hands—the sticks
And stones in the scrabbled air,
The water and light on the ground,
And nothing at all in mind.

Suddenly we're shut
Tight in a tight cloud.
It mills around us, grows
Thick as a gray beard
Through which, gusty and damp,

An incoherent wind
Breathes in and out of touch.
Then, jerked out by the roots,
It rises aslant and spills
Old Testament hailstones
Across what's left of us.
Sunlight breaks off, and lightning
Strikes like a blue law
As if to strike us dumb
Or scare us into our wits.
It doesn't. I love you.
But now we must climb down
Where everything, everyone seems
Under the old weather.

Fire by the River

We gather wood, the bleached, clay-covered branches
As heavy as fossils, drag them to the shore,
    And cross them, touching a match
To a nest of twigs. And the fire begins between us
Under this evening kindled by our breath.

It gathers dusk in tight against our backs,
Lighting us half by half. The river roars
    Like a fire drawn through a valley.
The smoke pours down to the water's edge like a creek
And empties into the broad, downstreaming night.

The first chill draws our arms around each other.
Like firelight under eyelids, the stars spread out.
    We lie down with ourselves.
The lighted halves of our bodies sink together.
The moon leans inward, banking on darkness.

Set free by our sleep and coming down to the water,
The bears, the deer, the martens dark as their fur,
    As soundless as night herons,
All drink and turn away, making no light.
The tail of the wind is stirring the soft ashes,

And nothing of ours will be left in the morning
Though we guard it now through dewfall and ground
        mist.
    But here at the heart of night
A salmon leaps: the smack of his wild body
Breaks through the valley, splashing our sleep with fire.

Nine Charms Against the Hunter

In the last bar on the way to your wild game,
May the last beer tilt you over among friends
And keep you there till sundown—failing that,
A breakdown on the road, ditching you gently
Where you may hunt for lights and a telephone.
Or may your smell go everywhere through the brush,
Upwind or crosswind. May your feet come down
Invariably crunching loudly on dry sticks.
Or may whatever crosses your hairlines—
The flank of elk or moose, the scut of a deer,
The blurring haunch of a bear, or another hunter
Gaping along his sights at the likes of you—
May they catch you napping or freeze you with buck fever.
Or if you fire, may the stock butting your shoulder
Knock you awake around your bones as you miss,
Or then and there, may the noise pour through your mind
Imaginary deaths to redden your daydreams:
Dazed animals sprawling forward on dead leaves,
Thrashing and kicking, spilling themselves as long
As you could wish, as hard, as game,
And then, if you need it, imaginary skinning,
Plucking of liver and lights, unraveling guts,
Beheading trophies to your heart's content.
Or if these charms have failed and the death is real,
May it fatten you, hour by hour, for the trapped hunter
Whose dull knife beats the inside of your chest.

In the Open Season

By what stretch of the mind had we come there, lurching
    and crackling
Mile after mile uphill through the ruts and ice-lidded
    chuckholes
On the logging road, the pine boughs switching across our
    windows?
It was the middle of gray-green daylight when we stalled,
    then climbed
On foot into scraggy clearings, while blue and ruffed
    grouse
Went booming and rocketing slapdash deep under the
    branches
Beside us, beating our hearts, and the guns began slamming
Their blunt, uninterrupted echoes from valley to valley.
We zigzagged up through the stunted hemlocks, over
    stumps and snow
Into shale, into light, to a ridgecrest frozen hard as a
    backbone
And, lying down as if breathing our last, caught the air
One burst at a time. When the world came back, we looked
At dozens of miles of it crumbling away from us
Where bears and deer were spilling out of hiding.
The overlapping thumps of shotgun and rifle
Froze us around each other out of the wind
Where frost had grown on itself, thicker than moss,
In spires and spikelets like a bed of nails
Under our backs by turns. And the light broke out
Of everything we touched in bristling spectrums,
And we felt the day break over again
And again, snow blowing across the sun
To dazzle our half-closed eyes.
But the earth shivered with guns
Below us—the birds, the bears,

And the deer bleeding toward sundown.
We touched each other's wounds
Like star-crossed, stir-crazed lovers
Dying again and again.

One for the Sun,
One for the Moon

Full of holes, the sunflower leaves
Are straining at the sun,
The flowerless stalk half grown.
Out of the alder grove
The hornets come again
To scissor with neat jaws
Another piece of a house
To hang in the ripe shadows.

Each black and yellow worker,
Mealing part of a leaf,
Flies mumbling out of sight
To make a moon in a tree
Where the darkness turns
As wild as hornets' eyes;
And the sunflower, day by day,
Takes riddling as it goes
Up to its burning head,
To its black and yellow answer.

Archeological Notes

Wherever they put their feet, the herdsmen beyond bleak
    Astrakhan
Scuffle in flint chips older than all arrows.
Past the concrete end of a runway in Seattle, bulldozers
    found
The sprawled, imponderable bones of a giant sloth.
Men stamping their feet for their lives in Rome have fallen
Down through the hollow streets to catacombs.
Under the flights of rain, clay dogs, clay men come
    tumbling
Into Oaxaca valleys like messages.
Digging for worms in Saratoga Springs, boys unearth
    muskets
And buckles, the green brass of revolutions.
In cities like kitchen middens, men crack the halves of
    themselves
And then go rich in a heap to be lived on.
Where I grew up—in a swamp east of Chicago—if you stamp
    your foot,
You stay right where you are and what you are:
Ditch-diggers in bogs and slag find nothing but Prohibition
    Man—
Thick skulls, gold teeth, and pointed preserved shoes.

Learning to Swim

Learning to swim meant watching from the shore
Good, grown-up swimmers laughing and diving
At the end of the broken pier, over my head.
They lay in the sun or waved at floating girls
Or dived into the water and came up shining
Out of high spirits like a school of fish.
I shrank from the water like my bathing suit
But went in anyway, wading as far
As my chin, rising on tiptoes at the last
But sinking back and turning.
There was no way out: nothing but jagged pilings.

One day, my feet came up by themselves. I crawled
Through the gray cross-waves, mouth shut water-tight,
Believing I would die from swimming badly
While the dry lifeguards, smiling up the beach,
Walked upside-down on the world with their bare
    hands.

As the watery raw air sank down my throat,
I saw the ladder, reached for it, held on,
And took the rungs as tightly as handshakes
But found myself alone on the platform,
Watching good swimmers start away from there,
All stroking idly through the afternoon
In the frank sunlight, calm on the surface,
To the impossibly distant rock whose light
Marked the horizon like the evening star.

The Warbler

My neighbor shut off his engine at the curb,
But as we talked, it started chirping and squeaking
Like a rusty ghost. We raised the hood and looked:
A half-grown warbler clung to a hood-brace,
Its beak still broad and yellow for feeding,
Gray-yellow powdered under its blunt wings.
If shifted tight to my finger, ruffled its down,
Then hunched and flew without a trace of a tail
All the way over the street, flew straight and hard
But downward, flopping and rolling
Finally among the roots of an elm.
I picked it up. It looked as good as new.

To make a story short, it died in the morning,
Having eaten nothing, having turned away
From eyedroppers and bugs on the ends of toothpicks,
Still chirping for something else we couldn't find
Like the nest it fell out of. My neighbor had driven
All over town that morning, noticing nothing.

I want to remember what we didn't see:
The warbler falling, for some damned reason or other,
And being fed or not being fed in the gutter
With a car stretched over it like a stormy arbor,
Then hopping from street to kingpin to shock-absorber
Over the fuel pump to a snarl of wires
To a slit of light where the hood and fender flange,
Jounced up and down, being waggled in a nest
Of pistons pecking their exploding chambers,
The horns in its ears like apocalyptic geese,
The engine roaring like a pterodactyl,
The endlessly belted fan whirling its wings
In the darkness. When those died down at our house,
It went on chirping its single demanding note.

The Scene of the Crime

At first, it seemed to be billing its reflection
As all ducks do, but the other head
Was right side up, dead-looking—no visible body
Where the neck led under water. There,
In the gunmetal gray daylight on the lake,
Like a washed-out photo of an atrocity
In a magazine, a duck was eating a duck.
Not putting anything past its appetite,
I watched the brown-headed, black-billed canvasback
Holding the soggy nape and a clump of feathers,
Swimming for shore, dunking and dragging
The limp, drab shape like a berserk lifeguard.

What else should they do with dead ones
After a fight? Or old ones, beaten by weather?
And *men* eat ducks. Or maybe someone had shot it
And this was the wildly sentimental rescue—
DRAKE SAVES MATE—for a Sunday supplement.

But then the surge of the superior tail,
The flurries among the coverts and folded wingtips,
Submerging and rising, woke me: they were mating.
I watched them rub it in, then break apart
To wash and preen in the polluted shallows.

Short Story

Description of young man standing outside the house
At night with insects and light effects, his nerves
Implied like the weather report by leaves and branches.
She lets him in with a flinch. Flat dialogue.
A dash of hands, a pinch of her face. He thinks
A quick montage of engagement. She leads the way
Upstairs through unnamed portions of his head.
A squeaking door-hinge. Father in bedroom corner
Covered with lint and mildew, Mother supine,
Her gray hair long as a nightgown. Extended pause.
Young woman bawling, Father scratching at cobwebs,
And Mother sinking in bed as if in a bath.

Description of young man catching his own eye
In mirror. Reflection. Self-hating metaphors,
Interior and exterior monologue,
Diction from high to slangy. Father and Mother
Begin harangue assisted by violins
With colored slides of doctors, lawyers, merchants,
And selected views of the Holy Land. Young woman
Falling down on the carpet, having a baby
Complete with sailor suit and pledge of allegiance
To the Stars and Stripes on bunting around the room.
Young man runs down and out, style going cold
As his breath. Description of patchy night. No comment.

From Hell to Breakfast

Leaving the night upstairs
And minding their manners,
They sit down at the table.
For what they are about
To receive, God, make them grateful
And good enough to eat.
What made these appetites?—
Tomato juice for vampires,
Heaps of scrambled eggs
While the rooster is still crowing.
And what's the use of letting
The night into the morning?
Stir sugar and cream in it.

Their eyes are the right colors
Except at the corners, their clothes
Are as cool as the season,
She put her face on straight,
He had a close shave, but they seem
To remember someone screaming.
Was it next door? In the street?
She dreamed something was burning
In the oven, a midnight snack
No one would dare to eat.
On stumps like a veteran,
Something walked in his sleep
Like himself cut down to size.

Give them their daily bread
And the daily paper. Hundreds
Were screaming if they had time:
Some fell or were pushed, and some
Ran smack into it

Or woke up behind bars.
Thousands coughed up their souls
In the night, and two got in
On the wrong side of bed
And cured their love like meat.

They both may be excused
If they wipe their mouths. Look,
No hands across the table, no
Holes in the walls, no windows
Scattered across the floor.
It could have been worse, and they
Could have been worse than it.
They have each other's names
On their shopping lists. In the doorway,
A brief passage of arms,
And they're off, they're off and running.

Weather Report

The north wind, like a fist,
Knocks numbly at the wall.
Snow deepens on the roof.
The draft through the empty keyhole
Is picking, picking its way,
And on the windows, frost,
That starry geometry,
Streaks out its axiom:
From nothing, nothing can come;
Persist, exist. My thought
Like a tongue on a hatchet
Sticks to its last cold proof.

Ceremony on Pier 40

No ships are shivering
These timbers. Like a wreck
They move with the littered chop
And backwash, muck and ruckus
Against the pilings. Nothing
Is coming or going. The idiot
Figurehead of the empty bollard
Weathers another morning.

Black wings held out to dry,
The dozing cormorant
Sits upright on a pole
Like a burnt flagstaff.
What does the mind do on a bad day?
Shrinking and cringing like a sea-slug,
It folds around its food,
It withers away from light.

At the edge, the game is called
Spit in the Ocean. Nothing shining
Rises to that bait.
The wind comes baffling east.
Now simply standing still
In the fog by the water
And holding on are enough.

Crossing Half a River

Stretching and heaving behind me, the snarled wilderness
Of crags as high as buildings, hanging valleys,
Paths cut by deadfalls,
And cracks where cedars cling for their lives, hogbacks and
     spurs
Where no one comes or goes by his own choice—
But here, an island in a river.
The shore, broadened by summer, shelves down to the
     quick water.
Hobbling, I come to the edge. A foot away
The fingerling salmon dart,
Then hover. In the riverbed the stones turn bright as birds,
Splashed, speckled like eggs or the breasts of fledglings.
Being shaken in my boots,
I start across as deep as my knees—hearing the rush
Of the milk-blue water coming down from snow—
As deep as my leaning thighs;
And the downstream leg must lead the way, groping and
     yawing
As it reaches ahead, the upstream leg coming level
In line with the current
For shelter. In the deep channel, this body—tilted,
     half-buoyant,
Unsure of itself, its feet at cross purposes—
Gives up its footholds lightly,
Halved by a horizontal storm and a vertical sun,
Head swimming with light and arms like stubs of fins
Fishing for balance.
Then slowly it finds itself: more surely the feet step down
On time pulled tight below them, not coming sideways;
They wallow ashore
On the downstream spit like castaways. The dividing river

Curves down its forks, riffling and whitening
Or smoothing deep in pools.
Far off, the upstream point is a jumble of head-sized stones,
But halfway here, on the spine of the bare island,
Gnarled by flooding winters,
Heaped with its own leaves, with the drifted rubble of
    seasons,
A clutch of willows like a broken garden
Begins living and dying,
Still separate, but slowly bringing a world together
With what can still be counted on my fingers,
With white-crowned sparrows
And mourning doves, with pipers and killdeer, with
    whatever
Comes to be caught at flood stage in the rains
When only the bent willows
Will keep their place above the crest of the river,
    beginning—
Like all I wanted to say—with sticks and stones
When thought first stuttered
Against the current. I recognize myself by the water,
Now going into the water toward the shore,
Now dreaming myself across.

Stretching

Leaving the road and crossing the hard shoulder
And walking on washed-out clay, having to zigzag
From sage to bunch grass to prickly pear to bones
A half-mile over the prairie to a butte
The size of a ruin—(the sun is crackling sideways
As straight, as dry, as thick as the wind
That's fallen flat on the ground this evening)—

In the wrong clothes, at the wrong time of day,
I come to the crumbling limestone foot:
There's no way up but up the pitching chimneys
Thirty rough feet to the crest. I climb them, passing
A disembodied rattle between rocks
Which means keep going or don't keep going,

And then I'm standing somewhere in Montana
South of Lame Deer, raw kneed, raw handed,
In a place I couldn't invent, in an old place,
On the sparse grass untouched by buffalo,
On table-rock half eaten by weather, the black-

And-white lark buntings skimming past stones
Heaped in a head-high cairn in the middle of nowhere,
Where someone came and waited once, then changed
Into wind and rain, into grass, sunlight, and dirt,

Which come and go, crossing each other out
In a heap as permanent as a landscape,
A place to be promised something bleak as years,

Where my hands and knees feel ready for a change,
Where giving up is perfectly natural,

Where giving back goes far as the eye can stretch.

Last Look

for Vernon Watkins—d. Seattle,
Oct. 1967

He was crossing a bridge when I saw him last,
A pack on his back, his gray hair glistening
In the rain. He was looking toward the mountains
Where the salmon in the channel under his feet
Were going that gray October.
His pack was full of books; he was starting home,
Eyes turning against the current toward high snow
As clearly, as naturally
As the eyes of the homing salmon under him.

Speech from a Comedy, II

Scene: The wreckage of Heaven

God must be master in his own house,
And if that means firing servants and wiping out stains and
    exterminating vermin, that's the way it goes.
We all have quirks and personality flaws.
      Chorus   His eye is on the sparrows.
I remember Heaven as it used to be:
A permanent, respectable, fashionable palace of jade and
    porphyry
Where nothing was boring and everyone listened to me.
      Chorus   God is a mystery.
It's hard enough to be God, let alone a full-time supervisor
Of every inch of earth, air, fire, and water.
I'm tired of squeezing into a glass of wine and a stale wafer.
      Chorus   God goes on forever.
I can still fly, I can move on the face of the waters, I can make
Thunder and lightning with a flick of the wrist. For God's sake,
How can Everyman possibly give *me* a headache?
      Chorus   God is not a joke.
I used to enjoy him. I could hear his prayers
And smell the charcoal-broiled offerings drifting up the back
    stairs.
Now all I hear and smell is General Motors.
      Chorus   God's not taking orders.
I don't like Death any more than the next man:
He's always interrupting and he smells to high Heaven.
But somebody's got to take out the garbage and empty the
    bedpan.
      Chorus   God is out of tune.
We all make mistakes, but I made a lulu
When I stranded the Ark and let everybody go.
I should have drowned old Noah and started a zoo.
      Chorus   God is turning blue.

I didn't ask for this job in the first place.
Theatrically, Heaven and Earth are a dead loss.
I said, "Let there be light" not "Let there be egg on my face."
   Chorus God is out of office.
I quit. I resign. Why, it's a miracle
I still have all my faculties from temple to temple.
If Everyman wants a King, he can go to Hell.
   Chorus God's the Golden Rule.

Note from Body
to Soul

Each word a rock
The size of a fist—
I throw them one by one
At the dark window.

Plainsong for Everyone Who
Was Killed Yesterday

You haven't missed anything yet:
One dawn, one breakfast, and a little weather,
The clamor of birds whose names
You didn't know, perhaps some housework,
Homework, or a quick sale.
The trees are still the same color,
And the Mayor is still the mayor, and we're not
Having anything unusual for lunch.
No one has kissed her yet
Or slept with him. Our humdrum lives
Have gone on humming and drumming
Through one more morning.

But for a while, we must consider
What you might have wished
To do or look like. So far,
Thinking of you, no one has forgotten
Anything he wanted to remember.
Your death is fresh as a prize
Vegetable—familiar but amazing,
Admirable but not yet useful—
And you're in a class
By yourself. We don't know
Quite what to make of you.

You've noticed you don't die
All at once. Some people like me
Still offer you our songs
Because we don't know any better
And because you might believe
At last whatever we sing
About you, since no one else is dreaming

173

Of singing: *Remember that time*
When you were wrong? Well, you were right.
And here's more comfort: all fires burn out
As quickly as they burn. They're over
Before we know it, like accidents.

You may feel you were interrupted
Rudely, cut off in the middle
Of something crucial,
And you may even be right
Today, but tomorrow
No one will think so.
Today consists of millions
Of newless current events
Like the millions of sticks and stones
From here to the horizon. What are you
Going to miss? The calendar
Is our only program.

Next week or next year
Is soon enough to consider
Those brief occasions you might rather
Not have lost: the strange ones
You might go so far
As to say you could have died for:
Love, for example, or all
The other inflammations of the cerebral
Cortex, the astounding, irreversible
Moments you kept promising yourself
To honor, which are as far away
Now as they ever were.

The Apotheosis of the Garbagemen

And they come back in the night through alleys to find us
By the clashing of raised lids,
By garage doors' lifted heads, the swung gates, the bottomless
Galvanized cans on their shoulders,
In luminous coveralls
They follow the easy directions on boxes, scattering
Bushels of brown grass and apple cores,
Old candy wrappers folded around sweet nothings,
And sacks with their stains on fire,
They are coming through hedges, dragging geometry
In a dark clutch of rainbows,
See, the smashed jars
Prinked out with light, and the vacuum bags
Bursting their dust in the night like the phantasms of horseflies,
Through the burning bacon fat
Their baseball caps go flying, their feet
As solid as six-packs on the lawn, the slam-bang of their coming
Sending the lettuce leaves against our windows
Like luna moths, the marrow whistling
Out of the wishbones of turkeys, the husks and rinds,
The lost-wax castings of corncobs and teabags,
The burnt-out lightbulbs pulsing in midair,
The coupons filled out
With our last names for all the startling offers,
Oh see, their hands are lifted by the gloves
Untying the knots in plastic bags, to catch
The half-burnt ashes raining around their heads,
The crusts and empties.
As the skeletons of lampshades catch at the first light,
They are going back in their empty trucks and singing
To the dump, to the steaming rust
In the rolling, hunch-backed, beckoning earth,
The sea of decay where our foundering fathers

Rubbled their lives,
They have found the way
Back to God's plenty, to rags and riches,
But will come back to us with all we could wish for
In the darkness, singing love and wild appetite,
The good rats and roaches,
The beautiful hogs and billygoats dancing around them.